*This book is dedicated to the memory of
the many who perished in the Holocaust,
and to the few Righteous Ones who helped
some survive.*

*This book is also dedicated to the author's
husband, Marek Kaplan, ("Tom" in the book)
and to her children and grandchildren.*

# Contents

. . . . .

# Prologue to the Past

· · · · ·

My family was my life, my home, my security. Only thoughts of them sustained me during the long years of war — my adored sister who was only a memory even then; my father, whom I worshipped; and my mother, whom I dearly loved, though not with the same degree of adoration I felt for my father. One day in 1969 I came upon a letter my mother had written to me in 1943 when she thought she was about to be deported and killed. When I read this letter, I was stunned. I realized I had never truly known my mother. I felt that I did not deserve to be her daughter. Why did she affect me so much more deeply in a letter that day, than in the years when I was growing up?

She died here in this country on November 24th, 1969, the date of my father's birthday who had died ten years earlier. I thought to myself that somehow my father had arranged it this way, to have her die on his birthday, because he could not bear to see her suffer so much. Was it a gift of God to my father or mother on this day? My mother's birthday was November 21st, and because it was so close to my father's, they used to celebrate them both together. My father would always give my mother red roses that came all the way from Lwow as there were no roses in Boryslaw in November. My sister and I would bring them to her in bed early in the morning, and always behind us was my father, smiling. Sometimes the roses would arrive wilted, but it did not matter. Roses in November meant so much in Boryslaw.

For years, company would come on November 24th, and they would dance, and laugh, and bring beautiful presents: Mosan crystal in all colors which my mother liked so much and many boxes of chocolates my sister and I adored. The house with all the lights aglitter seemed to us children, a fairy land.

This November 24th, 1969 was different. My mother died in a nursing home completely paralyzed and unable to speak. Only her eyes spoke, her large, deep black eyes which sparkled like stars when I was a child. They were so desperately sad during those last months.

Weeks later I went through my mother's belongings. There, in one drawer of her chest was a small blue-gray flannel bag pulled together with a black silk cord. Inside was a small pack of letters and documents. How old these papers were! My mother's diploma from a Vienna business school, her high school report cards. I thought how much these mementos must have meant to her, for her to try to save them from destruction during the long war period. She had never spoken to me or my sister about her business diploma, yet it must have meant a great deal to her to have kept it all her life. This was a part of my mother who died really unknown to me. And then there was this other letter written to me dated 27 May 1943.

I read it with tears streaming down my face at so much love, so much goodness! This was a letter written by a mother who thought at the time that she would be deported or killed at any moment, and these were to be her last words of advice to me. In a few hours or the next day she was supposedly going to be killed by murderers who had already murdered nearly all of the people who were dear to her, slaughtered for one reason only, that she and they were Jews, and she was telling me in this letter:

"I would very much like you to study, I would wish that you were able to use your abilities to do well for yourself and others. You are a true daughter of your father. Try to be as good, righteous, and giving of yourself as he is . . ." The hell which surrounded my mother, the bestiality of the Germans who killed little children, old people, and hoped to eliminate all Jews, the seeming indifference of other races of people who saw it happen—all this did not change her attitude towards life or towards other human beings. What she hoped would guide my life would be "goodness, righteousness, and generosity like my father." She wanted me to study and to help others. How could she still be thinking this way? She did not tell me how to survive or how to kill others in order to do so. What would I say to my daughter in a similar situation? What did the Germans tell their children before they went to Poland? To be good, righteous, and giving? My mother ended her letter to me, in these words, "if you are not a professional woman, then be a good housekeeper".

I tried to understand what prompted my mother to say this. I think she felt that she had failed my father. He used to say, whenever there was a party, that our mother acted like a guest in her own home. We thought he meant that she was so gay and happy to be having a party, but I think that she was hurt. She felt she had let him down. This sense of failure must have lain deep within her, that she should have written, at this crucial moment of her life, that I should be a good housekeeper if I did not have a career! How intensely she must have believed that her death did not matter and that I would survive—good and perfect in a perfectly good world.

# 1

. . . . .

# Boryslaw Before the War

Boryslaw was a town of about 40,000 people dominated by the oil industry. It was a dirty place; its grime was caused by spilled oil pouring through ditches and forming iridescent circles of green, blue, gold and black. These circles would develop into elipses and disperse into free-form shapes, only to become circles again. I used to watch the muddy water of our river, Tyśmienica, into which the oil would find its way, only there it would move faster over the flowing water while the patterns shaped and reshaped themselves in seconds. We would throw little stones into the water to break up the circles of oil and watch them reform. The odor of oil also permeated Boryslaw as one approached the town, but somehow we did not notice it for it would mix with the scent of our roses, linden trees and jasmine.

The roads in Boryslaw could not be paved as the pipes ran across and underneath the roads from wells to large silver containers. The pipes were continually in need of repair because they invariably got clogged. The roads were muddy in the spring and fall. In the summer the mud turned to clouds of dust raised by horses with buggies and an occasional car. In the winter the roadways were covered with deep snow and the buggies would be replaced by sleds, often pulling skiers close to the slopes of the

1

mountains. The sidewalks consisted of wooden boards higher than the roads but full of holes, conducive to breaking one's legs.

Oil wells were everywhere, behind the houses, over the hills and in the woods. Their wooden towers enhanced the town's horizon, surrounded by the foothills of the Carpathian Mountains. When we had nothing special to do, we would ask Wojtaszek, our coachman, to take us for a ride into the hills, over roads cut through pine woods. While sitting comfortably in a carriage or sled, depending on the time of year, we would plan our future, dreaming about all the beautiful things young girls do. Life was rosy and so beautiful. My only concern was that perhaps it might become too dull.

My mother had four sisters and a brother, my father, two brothers. Ours was a happy, extremely close-knit family. We would often meet, usually in our house in Boryslaw or in Vienna at my mother's parents' home. On holy days like Passover we always met at my father's parents' in Wolanka, a section in Boryslaw. There would sometimes be as many as twenty-five people gathered there, laughing and joking and trying hard to be serious when some prayers were read. But no one minded when we laughed, even then. From my grandparents my older sister Doneczka and I would get little gifts for returning the "afikomon" on Passover, or for birthdays or Hanukah. Those were usually golden earrings with shards of emerald or rubies, or small gold rings with tiny precious stones. We were supposed to keep them for our children after we outgrew them, but they somehow found their way to other children. We were not too religious, but our grandparents were. My parents would go to temple during our New Year and the Day of Atonement. I remember attending as a small child, finding it somewhat bewildering, and never asking to be taken again. Then when I attended Gymnasium, we had to go to services on all state celebrations, such as the birthday of the President, May 3, Constitution Day, or November 11, the celebration of Poland's independence. We usually sat together, a few close girl friends, whispered, giggled and hardly paid any attention to our professor of religion who conducted services for the Jewish students.

However, all the holidays observed by our family were very meaningful to me and my sister. Even today they are indelibly etched in my memory. Of course, the observance of Passover was the best. Aunt Zosia and Walterek would visit from Lwow, and rather often other sisters of my mother, Gizela or Judith, would arrive from Vienna.

It was also in Vienna that my mother went to school and where she matriculated from an advanced business academy. After she graduated, my mother worked for a top executive in the general offices of the oil industry and later was moved, with the whole firm, to Boryslaw in Poland. There she met my father, a young but extremely able, energetic and ambitious administrative manager, who would advance, in a short span of years, to a leading position in Boryslaw's oil industry.

Both of my parents would often speak about their childhood and their grandparents. I loved to hear those family stories. My father's ancestors were the rabbis of Breslau. Then they moved to Przemysl, where my great-grandfather also served as a rabbi. He was the author of books in Hebrew which could be found in the larger libraries. We always referred to him as our great-grandfather, "the writer." My great-grandmother, as a young girl, attended a priory, a private Catholic school in Przemysl, and spoke fluent French. Nevertheless, she raised her children, including my grandfather, in the strict Jewish tradition in accordance with the wishes of her husband, the rabbi. However, her only daughter married a Christian and was considered an outsider in the family. It was not until the war started, when the family wanted to find her to ask if she could hide my sick grandfather, that I discovered this family secret. No one knew her married name, so the attempt to locate her did not succeed.

Both my grandfathers were small merchants. My mother's father also worked in the Chancellory offices of the Kaiser in Vienna, as my grandfather would proudly claim, during the First World War. He received an honorary Order from the Kaiser, again as he would tell it, for his good work. This Order was his proudest possession, and he loved to show it to us. My mother and her family moved to Vienna right at the onset of the First World War. Before that, they all lived in Drohobycz, not far from Boryslaw. Both families, that of my father and mother, were of modest means, but they managed to educate their many children. As long as I could remember, my grandfathers were retired and were supported comfortably by their sons and daughters. They would spend their summers at the spas of Czechoslovakia. When my grandfather from Vienna went to Franzensbad for the thirteenth time, the mayor of the village greeted him at the station accompanied by an orchestra. He was so proud when he told this to us. My grandmother usually went to Marienbad, and my father's parents to Karlsbad or to Krynica or Iwonicz in Poland. That was their pleasurable routine, and it was the joy of their children to afford to give it to them until the advent of the Hitler era.

I hardly remember the house in which I was born—our "old" house—but I can still see in my mind's eye, the large chestnut trees which formed an alley in the middle of the large lawn where we played croquet and turned somersaults. When I was still very young, we moved to our "new" home. And our "new" home it always remained, with its red brick, tiled roof and white stucco walls. An architect originally built it for himself; but after his seventeen-year-old daughter died of tuberculosis, he sold it. It might have been a bad omen, but of course we could not foresee it as such. Some other people owned it for a short time and then we obtained it. It was one of the nicest houses we had ever seen. We had a board on which were numbers. It was downstairs near the kitchen, and when we rang the bell the maid would know which room was calling for her. As children we would have a marvelous time ringing and watching as the numbers popped out. We had an inside phone connection from our bedroom upstairs directly to my parents' bedroom downstairs in case we were frightened at night. We never used it except as a toy for and, finally, it was disconnected.

We employed two maids: a cook; a chambermaid who wore a uniform when she was serving; a coachman, Wojtaszek, who lived with his family in a wooden house in our back yard; a watchman who also took care of our yard and the dogs; and a chauffeur. Only the maids were paid by us; the others were on the payroll of the oil company where my father was the Administrative Director. Every second Sunday each of our servants had a free afternoon from one to seven p.m. We were not allowed to be even alone in the afternoon without the presence of one of the girls. What if we wanted some lemonade or cocoa for an afternoon snack? On one of our trips, while in a small hotel in Juan-les-Pins in southern France, we noticed that the owners ate with the help at one table and that the guests shook hands with the employees on departing from the hotel. That definitely was not the custom in Poland.

Socially ours was really a medieval society. Our coachman would sometimes wait for hours in winter for my parents to be driven home from a party. He would seat them in horse drawn sleds, bundled up in enormous sheepskin coats, sometimes even falling asleep in a sitting position. Shortly before the war my father had a phone installed in Wojtaszek's house and would call him to avoid the long hours of waiting. But it was still a primitive society.

My father was one of very few Jewish executives in the Polish oil industry. In the late twenties he was entrusted with the task of consolidating all the oil companies in Boryslaw into one amalgamated group, and then he became its Administrative Director. He was very young then. My mother recalled how he tried to make himself look older by growing a mustache. But with his light blue eyes and blond hair he would create the impression of being a youngster. It all understandably changed many years later when he began to look so much older than he really was. The owners of the company were all French, but the Polish government managed the oil wells for them.

Our home was furnished for comfort. I liked our oriental rugs best—most of all the dark Bokhara in my father's study and an orange one which covered the floor of the entrance hall. It was cut off in an unfinished rough way on the side near the wall. We were told that this was done by the Tartars who covered their carriages with it. We loved the story, and my parents never had the rug fixed—it was supposed to be a family heirloom, so the only problem was that both my sister and I wanted it.

Upstairs we had only Kilim coverings which we really liked, light beige with a geometric green, blue and rusty pattern. The upstairs area belonged to my sister and me. Our rooms were the nicest in the house. Our bedroom furniture was lacquered in pale green. We chose the style of beds and closets we wanted after we outgrew our brass "junior" furniture. A local carpenter custom built them with great care, as he did the furniture in our study which he painted a dark blue. Our bathroom was pink and very large as it was installed in an attic room. There we spent many hours reading in the bathtub and beautifying ourselves at the large double mirrors. The commodious upstairs hall contained a table at which we would eat when we had our friends over. The low windows around the staircase in the upstairs hall led to the lower one through which we could peek when my parents entertained. We would sit there, often until midnight, observing the guests. From our bedroom the doors opened to a terrace where we would sun bathe to our hearts' content.

To the left from the upstairs hall was the guest room which my aunts used when they visited us. We would talk with them for hours on end when we were supposed to be fast asleep. They were really our best friends, especially Judith, the younger one.

We got our milk from our two cows cared for by the coachman's wife, but it was the night watchman, Auslander, who I always associated with milk. Auslander came to us when I was about five years old. I can remember something of the many family discussions that led to our hiring this feeble old Jewish man, especially since my mother would have preferred a strong young Pole to watch our house. But my father's arguments prevailed: "If those who could hire a poor, unemployed Jew didn't, then who will?" So Auslander became part of our household, something between a fool and a tender, appreciated old man.

Auslander represented a kind of very religious poor Jew, a genre which was almost unknown to me. He was bearded and wore a black coat and hat. Every evening when he arrived he would come into the kitchen to tell the maids that he was starting his duties. By this time, my sister Doneczka and I were already in our nightgowns, ready for bed. When Auslander saw us, he would ask, "Have you said your prayers yet?" During the first week after his arrival, he taught us a Hebrew prayer, "Shaday Meshmireinu umacileinu micol Ro," which we were supposed to repeat three times. Then he would pick us up and let us kiss the mezzuzah that was attached to one of our doors. That virtually became a daily ritual. Although this practice lasted only a short while, I remember it clearly—Auslander picking me up to kiss the mezzuzah and I repeating the prayer word for word without having any idea as to what it meant.

Poor Auslander's tenure in our household did not last long. He tried his best but it seemed that he had two left hands and two left feet, as my mother often told us in desperation. He was not conversant with Polish, but attempted to speak German to us, as this language was closer to his native Yiddish, and both my sister and I understood German. Once he brought us a fish and called it a "fush." He looked at my mother in bewilderment when she asked him why he changed the word to "fush" when it was "fish," in both Yiddish and German. All he wanted, he said, was to speak proper German to the Frauleins so he assumed the word must be different from the Yiddish. We laughed and giggled for a long time. "Poor Auslander," we would sigh, "poor, poor Auslander."

One of Auslander's duties on his way to his home each morning was to deliver two cans of milk to my grandparents in Wolanka. The milk, of course, came from our cows, collected by the coachman's wife. The full cans were not especially heavy, but they were too much for the frail Auslander. He devised a strategy of his own to solve this problem. He would carry the two cans out of our house. Then, a few meters from our garden, he would set one can down on the edge of the sidewalk and carry the other one across the bridge to Wolanka Street where he put it down at the side of the road. Then he would go back over the bridge to retrieve the first can. Finally, with both cans in his arms, he proudly delivered the milk to my grandparents' home.

This routine worked well until one day when some kids, who must have observed him, took the cans, one at a time, when he wasn't looking. When he returned to our side of the bridge, the first can, of course, was gone. Then he rushed across for the second one and it too, had disappeared. Almost in tears, Auslander returned to tell my mother what had happened. From then on, the milk was delivered by our coachman, but this misadventure captured for us the other-worldly-like essence of our Auslander. He was not cut out for a hard life full of thieves and mischievous boys.

He disappeared from my life before I knew how to read or write, but the little prayer he taught me has remained with me ever since. I thought of it often throughout my life still without really knowing what it meant, and perhaps that is what made it magical for me. I remember repeating it to myself in the concentration camp, on the train bound as a laborer for Nazi Germany and on the ship that brought me to the United States. Years later my husband translated the short prayer for me: "Almighty God, protect me and save me from all evil." Was this all it meant? Nevertheless, those simple words encompassed all I ever really wanted, hoped for, and needed in those crucial moments. Even if the mystery was solved, once the words were clear, I still wondered. How could Auslander have known that someday I would need God so badly? The shadow of this frail man in his long black coat, black hat, white face, and reddish beard will remain with me forever.

One day while at the Eastern Fair in Lwow, my parents bought a "Centrefuga," a machine which would separate milk into heavy cream, light cream and skim milk. This became our favorite occupation. The machine was placed in an alcove on the side of the hall. Once when my parents celebrated my mother's birthday at a party which lasted until early morning of the next day, fresh milk was brought in, and all the guests tried our new machine.

Our dining room could seat many people with wooden planks added to the table. We loved to watch the preparations of beautiful lace tablecloths on the tables and the cobalt blue china. Every day, it was set without our assistance. At our main meals we had to finish everything that was served, from calf brains in shells for hors d'oeuvres, to spinach cutlets which we heartily disliked. When we really hated a dish, and in order to avoid a big argument, we would excuse ourselves by feigning headaches. To feed us properly was the chief concern of my mother. We had our yearly medical checkups by Professor Grer, a pediatrician in Lwow. He would fluoroscope our lungs as tuberculosis was an imminent danger in Poland, and he would prescribe the right food if he found us too thin. Interestingly enough, his regimen was more French than Eastern European—spicy sandwiches with sardines and anchovies, lots of lemonade with half a lemon, and not too much milk. My mother followed all his orders scrupulously, whether or not they made any sense to her. With all this wonderful care we still suffered from constant colds, especially me. It was chiefly for this reason that my mother took us on two-month trips every summer and winter travels during Christmas vacations. The change of air was considered quite important. First, a month at sea, then the mountains. It was a very pleasant ritual.

We had a governess at home from the time I was six years old. Our nanny was a German lady whom we called "Loyla." Our first one was a Russian refugee named Dina who spoke with us only in French. Russian was not a language then that people were anxious for their children to learn. She did not leave any lasting impression on me except that I remember she would fry sardines which to this day I always connect with Russian gastronomic affinity.

A few years later Miss Lusia, a marvelous governess, was hired. She was an artist who graduated from the art academy in Berlin and who spoke fluent French and German. My interest in art probably started then. She would show us how to model things that came from the earth that Wojtaszek, our coachman, dug for us from around the river. She could draw beautifully with black ink. Still, the best at pastel drawing was my Aunt Giza. I would watch her for hours when she was sketching cyclamens. We called them Alpine violets. It was through her that my love for art was to dominate my life.

My sister, Doneczka, played the piano when she was quite young. She was very talented and showed great promise at a very early age. She played in all the recitals at school. I took lessons for only a year. I realized even then that I could never be as good as my sister. I suffered from migraine headaches since childhood, and I always managed to have one when our piano teacher arrived. The same thing would happen when our Hebrew teacher called. I do not believe that my Hebrew education lasted longer than six months.

I loved our dogs most of all. First we had Dosiak, a gray German shepherd, then three more of the same breed: Nero, whose one ear would not stand up, and two handsome specimens, Jake and Miki. Later we acquired a Doberman, Dingo, of whom I was slightly scared. My most beloved dogs were Grom (Thunder), a St. Bernard, and Kajusek, a grown dachshund who usually slept at my feet. I remember once my father threw Kajusek outside when he wet the rug in his study. It was teeming and my sister and I were sure that he would never survive the rain. Kajusek whimpered outside, and Doneczka and I sat at the door inside and cried. An hour passed before my father relented. He could be very stern at times.

My whole life revolved around my dogs, my two deer who lived in an enclosed part of our garden, my rocks that I collected from childhood and a little later, wooden boxes and other utensils crafted with beads by Ukrainian peasants. I kept them all upstairs in our study and bedroom and would look for hours at the colored beads' designs. I also collected elephant charms. When I had twelve of these, my Uncle Leon bought one. I stole the elephant from him. That was supposed to bring me a great deal of luck. Throughout my life I thought about that. Was I really more fortunate and if so, was it due to the thirteen elephants, the stolen last one?

Our Uncle Lonek was a bachelor when we were children. When he was not in Vienna but in Boryslaw to attend to his oil wells, he would visit in the evening and tell us a story, which went on and on. Each evening's tale was a continuation of the same theme—it dealt with the life of a family of bears. Even if he went away for a long time, he would remember where to pick up the story, or at least that is what we thought. We adored him, and Doneczka was definitely a star in his eyes until she died.

On rare occasions Uncle Ludwik, my mother's younger brother, would visit us. He was very handsome and always well-groomed. One day when he arrived, and before he greeted us, he straightened a package of chocolates which was lying on a small table in the hall. He folded the silver paper around it, and only then did he turn to us with a big smile and a kiss. I was always a little afraid of him as he was a physician, and physicians always seemed to terrify me from the time I was very small. Ludwik would also ask us embarrassing questions about whether we were taking cold showers each morning, which he considered the best precaution against colds, and he also wanted to know if we ate a half grapefruit each morning. According to him this was essential. We hated both. That was our uncle then, as I remember him, always orderly, always caring, always loving.

I skied from the age of seven, not expertly. My friends were better, but I enjoyed it immensely. I was, however, good at throwing the disc, a wooden disc with metal edges and a metal center. After I took a few practice throws, the disc would soar far and high. I also loved to swim and swing. We had a large swing in our back yard, a bar and rings, and a ping pong table. I loved those things. That was my life. Any my blue bike on which I rode around the grass and roses in our garden. We had 400 red roses and some beautiful yellow ones, but we were not gardeners. My father was the only one who truly enjoyed it. He derived his greatest pleasure from cutting the grass with a scythe when he had the time, which was seldom.

I adored my father but I was scared of him. He was so important in town. I loved my mother and all my aunts as well. Of all my cousins, I was closest to Walterek who was only a year and a half my junior. But to girls, traditionally so much more mature, he always seemed like a baby, especially to me. When he was very little, he would call tea "pilaten" and chocolate "lepta"—words which had no meaning in any language. He was beautiful with large black velvety eyes, a quiet boy, sweet and gentle. Doneczka and I would tease and scare him by telling him about haunted places in our cellar. His mother, my Aunt Zosia, married Heini, a Czechoslovakian. from a very wealthy family that owned a textile factory in Brno. Walter, from childhood, was primed to take over the factory some day. He spoke German and Polish fluently and attended the German Evangelic Gymnasium when he was twelve years old. It was decided that he should study textile engineering while in college. Everything was planned so precisely, but it worked out much differently. My Uncle Heini died in his mid-thirties and was buried in Vienna. Doneczka passed away later and was buried in the same cemetery. Their graves are near each other.

My Aunt Zofia managed quite bravely as a widow. She received a pension which left her financially comfortable, and she loved her Czech family. We often visited her in Lwow. I loved to look at her because she was always so well-dressed, with attractive accessories, in unique combinations. She was, however, painfully unsure of herself. When she had parties my mother sent her baked pastries. She would also prepare a list of topics she could introduce in the event the conversation at her dinners lagged or did not proceed smoothly. Everything was planned meticulously for each day; yet, when her life crumbled, she managed quite well.

For as long as I can remember, Antosia was my aunt's maid. When I was a child she taught me to tie a handkerchief around a chair leg and to say a prayer to St. Anthony, her patron, if I lost anything. This was supposed to facilitate finding the misplaced object. I still do it to this day.

Zosia would arise every morning to prepare breakfast for Walterek, then she would take a bath and go back to bed. By noon, beautifully attired, she would visit with friends in one of the coffee houses of Lwow. Usually it would be in the Roma or the St. George Hotel, or if she were in a hurry, the Zalewski where they served the best coffee, or at the Teliczkowa for the tastiest little sandwiches. Whenever my mother, my sister and I came to Lwow to shop, we joined her. There were no coffee shops in Boryslaw, and it was always a treat for us.

Zofia's apartment was small but tastefully furnished. Everything that she possessed was exquisite, every piece of Mosan crystal the most beautiful, as was her small collection of hand-blown glass animals. She kept all the colored ribbons from gift boxes she received in one crystal bowl. From the time I was a small child, I admired her hobby. She was as methodical as I was sloppy.

When Walterek was thirteen years old, I remember my mother mentioning that my grandfather from Vienna came to take Walter to the synagogue for a service and that he had bought him a gold watch. That was his "Bar Mitzvah," although, that it was so called, I did not learn until I came to the United States.

During our vacation trips abroad, most often to Italy, we would always pass through Vienna to visit my grandparents. When I was there, just before the invasion of Austria by Hitler, aunt Zosia also arrived with Walter. The two of us ran through the streets of Vienna. I took Walter to the two museums, the Kunst Historische and Kunst Gechichte. We spent so much time there that the guide disregarded our presence, and we did not have to pay for the "tours" he was conducting. It was in Vienna that I first saw the Titian painting of the "Gypsy Madonna." I was disappointed that Titian pictured her with black hair. My aunts always told me when I was very little that my hair was Titian. It was always my strong feature, the only one. Now I faced Titian's work depicting a black-haired woman, just when I was ready to check if my hair was really "Titian." My aunts worried very much about my appearance. My face was round, with just a hint of squareness, but then only long faces were fashionable. My neck was short, and only long ones were attractive, and, of course, I was short—and clothes would look more stylish on tall women. How was I ever to survive?

I considered Venice my home away from home. I loved the stands that displayed corals and Murano beads, the Doge Palace with its sad bridge where those condemned to death could see Venice for the last time, and the opulent women painted on many walls and ceilings. I recall that as a very small child my sister and I watched a little boat on the canal all covered with colored lanterns at night. We thought that it must have been a royal boat.

My mother often toured alone, usually she went to Baden near Vienna where she would stay in a sanatorium. It was a fashionable place; besides, her heart was slightly damaged after a rheumatic infection. She wrote fascinating letters about people she met. My sister and I were slightly upset that my mother would leave our father so often. But he never minded. He adored her as ever a wife was adored and strengthened her for the life which she was destined to live—almost as if he had a premonition.

In Boryslaw my parents attended many parties. My mother would have her clothes made in Lwow or Vienna, always very critically appraised by my father. At her own gatherings, according to my father, she behaved like a guest, having a grand time. My mother laughed a great deal. Once when we were in Krynica in a large hotel, my mother, sister and I, were having supper. Suddenly my mother started laughing at a remark my sister made. A lady who was sitting in the same dining room with her family came over, introduced herself, and said that she just had to meet my mother, because somebody who can laugh like that must be marvelous. The lady and her family were from Lodz and were cloth manufacturers. From then on we would often meet on vacations until it all unfortunately ended rather abruptly.

When I was eleven years old, my aunt Gizela married my father's brother, my Uncle Leon. Their wedding took place in our house, and I cried when I witnessed the ceremony. I still cry at weddings. The only one at which I did not do so was my own. When their son was born, my little cousin Oleś, his nurse would bring him to our garden and there in the shade of our trees he would sleep for hours. At times, we would come from Gymnasium, located on a hill just about five minutes from our home, to look at him during our recess. When he was older he would run after our animals. Every morning he would talk with my mother on the phone and ask, "Ami, the chickens, ducks and turkeys—are they still there?" My mother would answer, "They are all here, just come over." This went on for a long time and became part of a daily routine until he was three and a half years old—in fact, until the outbreak of war. And that was the picture of Oleś I kept in my memory throughout the war, and even to this day.

Our life was like a dream until my sister died when she was nineteen years old, and before the war. I loved that beautiful girl dearly. I could not talk about her death for years. It is difficult, even at present. During the war my mother, father and I would say, "Thank God Doneczka is not here, that she was spared from suffering through it all." I was sure that she would not have survived. I was the strong one.

All the parties at our house came to an abrupt end after my sister's death. On her gravestone in Vienna my parents had inscribed, "With you all our joy disappeared." We would visit Do-neczka's grave during Hitler's occupation of Austria. Her fiance would also come along. My sister died a month before they were to be married. He was a physician and planned to specialize in brain surgery in the United States.

Vienna was completely devastated, as if the people threw off their usual well-known "freundlichkeit." All those benches with signs "Juden verboten" (Jews forbidden) were unbelievable. We learned about those notices from newspapers and accounts of other people, but to actually see them was a tremendous shock. We walked through the streets and just stared. My grandparents were securely settled in Poland by then, in Drohobycz, a town eight kilometers from Boryslaw. Now when in Vienna, we no longer went to look at their home where we had all been so happy and where we spent so many glorious vacations. This all came to an end, but somehow the occupation of all of Austria by Hitler did not seem to affect us. When we met German refugees in 1938 in Genoa, Italy, on the way to the French Riviera, we wept with them but the enormity of the event still did not touch us too deeply. I remember two girls, about ten and twelve years old, who were in Genoa's port waiting for the ship bound for America. They were emigrating alone. Their parents were not allowed to leave. Even that did not make us think more clearly—we were still going to the Riviera for a vacation. The "Camichi Neri" de Mussolini looked strange but did not scare us, either. After all, those were the Italians with whom we spent so many summers. We seemed secure in our naiveté, so extraordinarily safe.

My parents wanted me to participate in all sports activities. When I was thirteen they allowed me to spend weekends skiing with my school friends in the nearby mountains, and to spend a night or two in tourist houses. My father broke his leg while skiing when he was in his late thirties, and that ended his career on the slopes. But when the snow was packed and the sun was shining, my father would permit me, when I suggested it timidly, to miss school and would send me out to ski with Wojtaszek.

It was in 1938 when I was in Zakopane, skiing during the school year when my Aunt Judith and I heard on the radio that Hitler occupied Austria and the text of his telegram to Mussolini, "Musso-lini, I shall never forget you," which referrred to Mussolini's approval of the German aggression.

I loved my father. No friend of mine was ever allowed to do what I did. Even now when I think about him in other contexts, I always return, in my thoughts, to my skiing expeditions, and I believe that he was the greatest of all fathers. When my sister and I brought our report cards home from school, we would get a kiss for every "C," not only for grades "A" or "B."

My father always told us to "try to do your best"—that's all he expected. He wanted me to study geology. He thought I would then literally have the whole world open before me, and he would always mention Persia. He took me with him to conferences at the geological station in our town, where I looked at the stones collected there, while he discussed with geologists where to dig for oil. But my affinity for geology ended after I took the course in Gymnasium. It was not the study of minerology, which I somehow expected, but the boring history of earth formations. One poor teacher of geology, and I decided that architecture would be my future profession.

When I was fourteen years old, during the winter months, I read John Galsworthy's *The Forsythe Saga* and Leon Trotsky's *Memoirs*, a strange twosome which gave me lots to think about. I read Proust when I was fifteen and listened carefully when somebody mentioned his books, as often happened, later during the war. We all read a great deal, and books tended to change our approach to life year after year. When I read Dostoyevsky I was depressed for weeks. Then Tolstoy became my beloved author, and Chekhov. The books I read then would color the events in our town and in my own life.

Always, for as long as I can remember, on May 1st the workers had a day off and they would march through the town singing. On this particular May 1st in 1938, Leszek, a boy friend and the son of an engineer, and I met on the street quite by accident, both eager to see what was happening. When the marching workers approached, we joined them. My heart pounded with excitement. They were singing and shouting that perhaps tomorrow all the world would be theirs. When they passed our house, they raised their hands in fists. It frightened me, but the experience was worth it.

My father smiled when I told him about my day. He was always interested in workers' movement. He was a democrat at heart, not a socialist.

My enthusiasm for the workers' cause was short lived. I remember sitting upstairs in my study and looking through the window at the men going to their shift on the job. They were dressed in dark oily clothes and wore caps like the coal miners did, though I had never seen a coal miner then. I looked at them and felt sad. What a dreary life, I thought.

Small incidents took place then which were probably always happening though I never paid any attention to them before. Our windows were opened in the winter for about half an hour daily when the house was being cleaned. One day I heard workers yelling as they passed in front of our house, "We are freezing and they open their windows for ventilation."

Another time when I took my usual ride in the carriage with Wojtaszek, a worker shouted something to the coachman of part of which I heard only ". . . can't they walk . . ." Wojtaszek hit the horses and we moved faster. Influenced by this event, with a few girl friends we decided to help the poor of our town. But first, we had to find these people. Somebody mentioned that they lived in houses right in the hills of the wax mine. We were horrified. We never believed that such poverty existed, and agreed to do something for these unfortunates. We would meet after school to knit scarves or sweaters. But I was the first to drop out. I had two left hands where knitting and sewing were concerned. My mother permitted me to take a bundle of my worn clothes to give to the people on the hill. Still feeling so deeply about their plight, I wrote a composition for our Polish class, "The Poor Ones in Our Town and What Are We Doing About It?" But by then, other projects superseded this one. I was never really socially minded.

My parents belonged to many philanthropic organizations. They contributed money but were not active. My mother was a "room mother" for my sister's class and accompanied the students on school excursions as a chaperon. I never wanted her to do this for my class. I preferred to go with the other mothers. My parents were not active Zionists, but they still recognized the importance of this movement. Interestingly enough, my mother was the first president of WZO in Boryslaw. It happened quite suddenly. One day an Englishwoman arrived in our town and asked my mother to form a local WZO group. I still remember my mother presiding over her first meeting to which both men and women were invited. She wore a beautiful suit, a new hat and used some rouge so as not to look too pale if she became nervous in front of all those who attended. On the advice of my father she took a tiny sip of cognac to buoy her spirits. That's all I remember about my mother's short term as President. Someone else succeeded her soon afterwards. I knew that some people were leaving for Palestine but I could not understand why anyone would want to go there. Palestine seemed too far away, like America! It seemed to me that people who went there were those who failed to succeed in Europe, but I never really thought too much about it. All of our friends were wealthy Jews as well as financially well established Ukrainians and Poles. Somehow I never did associate their desire to leave with nationality or religion. I felt that the people who were not succeeding at home should have tried harder.

Then my parents joined the B'nai B'rith. I was greatly impressed. Another family was also invited to join. They were the Shuzmans, and together they went to attend the installation dinner in Lwow. My mother bought a new long simple dress with a short bolero jacket, and my father wore a smoking jacket. Somehow, from my parents I got the impression that henceforth we would have brothers and sisters all over the world. Ironically, this assumption was very disappointing, but that came so much later, in the U. S. We probably expected too much or misunderstood the role of this organization.

My mother was also an active member of the Jewish Orphanage where poor Jewish girls were supposed to learn some kind of trade. Well intentioned as the plan was, only one girl succeeded. They were taught to sew. The attempt to train them to become good housekeepers, cooks and hotel personnel did not materialize. My father always preferred a sort of housekeeper-economy-husbandly like school for which Holland was famous. He wanted it for the poor Jewish girls in town. He also planned to send my sister and me, during, or after our studies to Holland for a year, to attend this kind of school so that someday we could become ideal housewives. This also did not succeed.

There was definitely a social dichotomy among the Jews, Poles, and Ukrainians in our town, but I felt comfortable in any group. Throughout my childhood, I never gave too much thought to the fact that I was Jewish or of any possible disadvantages this could incur. I wanted to be a boy rather than a girl, as boys could lead more adventurous lives. But I never had any wish to be a Christian rather than a Jew. Because of my father's position, I felt very secure, right at the top in our small town society. He would always caution us that being high up in Boryslaw did not necessarily mean being on top of the world. Out of our familiar surrounding, in a different environment, we would simply be nobodies, but this hardly had anything to do with being Jewish. My father also made this remark respecting wealthy Polish Christians who were also socially prominent in our town.

My parents' closest friends, who attended our "jours", as we called the days when bridge was played at our home or elsewhere, were mostly but not exclusively Jewish. They were owners of oil wells, lawyers and physicians. There were also some mixed marriage couples among my parents' friends but not too many. My mother and father also attended all the parties at our Jewish Community Center, where dances were held to raise money for local Jewish causes. In high school my closest friends were Jewish and Ukrainian, but it was a matter of coincidence that many of my sister's best friends were Polish Christians. All of the people we knew dated Jewish and non-Jewish boys, often equally. Still, certain teachers at the Gymnasium favored Polish students over Jewish ones. One of my Polish Christian colleagues, a quite mediocre student, said to a Jewish boy in the presence of a few other persons, "I know that you are much abler than I am, but it will be I who will be admitted to whatever school I choose, not you, just because you are Jewish." This statement affected me, but I still did not believe that being admitted to a particular school or qualifying for many others made a difference. I was certain that each one of us would find one school that would admit both of us. I further felt that being proficient made the crucial difference. That again was due to my parents' teaching, whose stated principle was "All that you can do is your best and to work hard, everything else will fall into place." I knew about anti-Jewish riots at universities in Poland and about the fact that Jewish students had to stand during lectures, refusing to sit on the left side. But since I was still in high school and planning to study abroad in the future, where children of my parents' friends usually attended schools, this fact was not of great importance to me. At this stage of my life it was irrelevant.

In contrast to large cities Boryslaw was intellectually a dull town, but books were available. The community boasted a library and a book store where we could order any volumes we wanted. In our study upstairs my sister and I had four hundred volumes which were catalogued and numbered, and our friends had about as many.

We subscribed to quite a number of papers and literary journals, such as "CHWILA," a Jewish daily written in Polish and published in Lwow, "Wiadomoscie Literackie," French magazines such as "Illustrations" and many others. Our travels enriched our lives tremendously. It was only then that we were able to appreciate a theater play or an opera. But the greatest stimulation was provided by my father and his brothers. Although, as children, we were not encouraged to participate in adult conversations, we were always allowed to listen.

As I look back on this period in time it now appears to me that my commitment to home and family might have been different had I been older when it all disintegrated. But at this juncture in my life it was my home which gave me the raison d'etre to survive the following very difficult years. It was enough for me then to close my eyes and envision my life in Boryslaw, my family, my treasures, my dogs, and my roses and trees. In later years I never felt poor even when I did not own material things. I always felt rich in a special way, superior to all other people. I suppose I inherited this belief from my parents. It was their greatest gift, one which no one could take away from me. It was my most prized possession then and now.

## THE OUTBREAK OF WAR—SEPTEMBER 1, 1939

I was standing at the corner of Pańska Street, our main thoroughfare, with a few other students of the private gymnasium of King Kazimierz the Great. From the loudspeaker we hear the somber voice of our president announcing that the war with Germany had started and that France and England would soon enter. I could not believe it! The big adventure was unfolding; and it was happening to me, not to my mother in 1914 or to my grandmother in God knows when. It was touching me right now! What is war really like, I asked myself. What will happen to our lives? How long will it last? Over and over again I asked myself these questions. Life was so boring in its peacefulness, and now this is supposed to be my great experience? Throughout my life I heard many stories about other wars, but about this one I will be talking to my children. I must see all of it. I should not miss anything. This is history in the making; and I am here to witness it, to participate!

I ran home to find that my father had just arrived also. He

brought masks to be worn against poison gas. We all expected this war to be fought with this deadly poison. We were so ineptly informed that we did not know when to wear the masks, when the sirens were sounding, or when the planes were soaring over us or when the gas actually reached us. Then we also realized something no one had thought of before—the masks were too large for Oles to wear. How could we use ours and let Oles die? While I was thinking about this problem, we ran to the basement with every sound of the siren and listened to the messages constantly repeated over the radio "going . . . coming . . ." None of us could understand a word. Not one plane passed over our town during that day.

On the following day my father had a shelter built between the trees in our garden. It was a deep hole in the ground buttressed by bags of sand piled in horizontal rows. After this project was finally finished, our whole family decided not to stay in Boryslaw but to move to Truskawiec, a small summer resort town about four miles from Boryslaw. We remained there for a short time, all four of my grandparents, my mother's sisters and their children. On the second evening we heard rumors that drunken bands of Ukrainian peasants were looking for Jews. We had a good idea about what would happen, but we did not take this story seriously—we were loathe to believe in rumors. When my father and his brothers arrived that night, we all moved back to our respective homes in Boryslaw.

Before leaving for Truskawiec, my mother, with the help of our watchman and maid, packed most of our silver into large boxes which we then buried in our back yard. We did not realize how much aggravation that would cause. Somehow we never anticipated the full dire consequences of our moves. But how could one foresee the changes that would occur in people during wartime? About a year later, the watchman and the cleaning girl, who were much closer friends than we thought, said they would denounce us for hoarding ammunition along with the silver if certain of their demands were not met. By that time, however, our silver was removed, but the marks of digging were visible for a long time. After much worrying on our part, the watchman and the girl took what they wanted—including boxes of fine Rhenish wine we had stored in the cellar for years. If only they had told us what they wanted at the beginning! We never saw them again.

At the outset of the war the owner of the local grocery suggested that we buy 50 kilograms of sugar he had managed to acquire. We all laughed it off—the war would never last long enough for us to consume so much of it. My Aunt Gizela was the only one who bought any supplies, especially soap. She stacked many boxes of beautifully colored Elida soap—her favorite brand—into her clothes. She certainly did not anticipate that all this aromatic bounty would be stolen by her maid. Again, we could not imagine all the social changes that this war would create.

We really did not know what to expect. If we did, we would have left Poland in the first days of September as my mother had wanted. We still had our car; we could have left for Romania or Hungary and from there on to England. My father was the one who objected. He did not want to leave the entire family. I suspect he was also interested in seeing how and what events would develop. In this respect I was very much like my father. We were both curious and did not want to miss any political action. History always fascinated us and here we felt we would witness and be part of it.

On a beautiful sunny day in mid-September, the German Wehrmacht entered our town without a shot being heard. My father was in his office confronted with many problems among the workers. They wanted to be paid, but by then the money for the payroll had been withdrawn by one of the directors who was supposed to send it to the company owners in France. Thousands of workers were standing around. My father was called to appease them. I was terrified and scared of large crowds then. He succeeded somehow, but we had little time to rejoice. The Germans had arrived.

An official in town phoned my mother to ask if she would permit the Germans to establish their headquarters in our house as it was sufficiently large and quite centrally located. She answered, "I have to call my husband at the office to ask him if it will be all right." That remained a joke in our family. We laughed about it for months until finally one could no longer laugh. The German soldiers arrived, put a few men on guard in front of our house which was displaying the Nazi flag. A few high ranking military men were also present. They introduced themselves and suggested that we put some covers over our Danzig table in the dining room and over our mahogany Biedermaier table in the salon as they were going to use the rooms for office work and did not want to ruin the highly polished expensive wood. We looked at each other in amazement. We expected almost anything, but not this politeness from the Germans. Events moved so rapidly as they usually did during wartime. General headquarters were established in our house in a matter of minutes. I stood by a window at the side of the house left for our use, and watched people enter and leave, men and women, probably local people whom I had never seen. One woman entered wearing a black veil that covered her entire face. I immediately suspected they were spies and collaborators—"Volksdeutsche" who had worked for the Germans before the war.

In the surrounding woods, Poles and Ukrainians were fighting. Rumors spread that the tongues of some combatants were cut out. I never did get these horrible stories straight. What irony. With German guards in front of our house we felt quite secure, even if only for a short time. So safe, that one Polish friend of my fathers asked if we would hide his son there because he was involved in Ukrainian-Polish fights. We kept him upstairs till the matter quieted down.

Then, according to a German-Russian agreement of mid-September, the part of Poland in which we lived was to be ceded to the Russians. We knew very little about all those political pacts and agreements. After a few days' stay, the Germans left Boryslaw. Just before they departed, my mother was in the garden near our roses. The German colonel approached her to say goodbye. He kissed her hand and said, "Gnadige Frau, we are not all barbarians." They got into their cars and left. Minutes later one of the autos was driven back and a young adjutant jumped off. He returned our car that he had used for water. This was a unique experience and that is how our first encounter with the Germans ended.

A few days later my father woke me at six in the morning. He received a call from the office advising him that a Russian patrol was seen behind a mountain. The Russians did not enter our town until the final days of September. By then the Polish "golden fall" gave way to rainy cold weather. From afar we could hear the sound of moving cars. All the church bells were ringing. I begged my Aunt Judith to accompany me to town to find out what was going on. We stayed at the curb of the road. It was teeming without interruption. The mud reached our ankles. A steady stream of Russian tanks moved through the streets for hours on end. I thought that many of the tank drivers were Mongolians and Tartars. They were grim looking, tense, and mistrustful. One of the tanks was driven by a pretty young woman. I could see her face for only a moment, then she disappeared under the top. They kept rolling on, the bells were ringing, and the rain continued to teem. That was our first day under Russian occupation. I did not know what to expect. I knew the Russia of Tolstoy, Dostoyevsky, and the sensitiveness and fatalism of the intelligentsia. I had also read the memoirs of Leon Trotsky whose popularity was already waning among the Russians. What would we have to face now? Who are those people in the tanks that were overrunning our town?

# 2

. . . . .

# Under Russian Occupation

## STILL IN BORYSLAW

The realization of the tremendous political changes which were to take place did not impact on me at first. Our entire family recovered quickly from the first day of shock and confusion, and even joked light-heartedly. My Aunt Otylia, whom we called Ila, was always the first to laugh. She, together with her husband and daughter, Elzunia, fled from the Germans in Krakow, to reach us. They left the shirt factory my uncle had opened after abandoning their first factory in Vienna in 1937. My uncle worked hard all his life. He was an extremely interesting man; an inventor. Every few years he would obtain a patent only to find out that something similar had been already invented. In general, it was difficult in Europe to succeed in his kind of career. Years earlier he pleaded with my aunt to move to America. But in our family we believed that the only people who went to America were probably misfits; people who could not succeed here. We were a closely knit family. Everyone helped one another to get established first in Vienna, then in Krakow. Now they reached us in a small Mercedes, bringing with them only the possessions they were able to pack into the car. All the machinery remained in Krakow.

My Aunt Ila was still always the first to laugh. That was one of the traits that her husband adored from the time they first met when she was only fifteen years old. Ila entered my room and laughing until tears rolled down her cheeks, said, "Everything that is mine is yours; what is yours is mine, and I am keeping this nice ring I found in the bathroom." We all laughed. Of course, when the Communists arrived, we became convinced that this their motto.

The same day we experienced this attitude in a somewhat different situation. A group of local girls, communist sympathizers, who hid their feelings until now—among them was the girl who was our manicurist and pedicurist—came and asked if they could cut our roses to place them in front of a picture of Majakowski. They did not even wait for our answer, but wilfully cut them. I could not believe it. Then, the manicurist, looking straight into my mother's face said "You will not be so important any more; we are taking over." She didn't realize that the Russians cared very little for pre-war Polish Communists and would deport them to Russia. There she stood facing us with an air of superiority, hate and defiance. All through the Russian stay in Boryslaw, my mother never visited a beauty parlor. She never wore a hat either. We all tried not to be conspicuous, naively thinking that this would help. At the beginning, the local Russian sympathizers were most difficult to abide. We knew them well but never expected so much hostility. Ironically, this often came from the poor Jewish workers whom my father had helped for so many years.

I disliked the Communist sympathizers. I resented their sudden negative approach to my father who, before the war, had overcome so many problems to keep them working. Whenever there were reductions in the ranks of the workers in the oil company, my father would not sleep nights knowing that those were the ones who he was supposed to fire. If he would not help them, who would? I was very young, looking at the world from a child's perspective, seeing everything through the safe windows of my secure world. I did not like what I saw. I would never try to understand anyone else's viewpoint, and would always view the world from my private ivory tower. I never realized how difficult it was for minorities to survive in the pre-war period. I lived in a circumscribed world, and I was holding on tenaciously.

The Russians needed my father. They appointed him as general manager of the oil industry in the eastern and western regions of previously Polish Ukraine. My father often attended conferences with their dignitaries and once with a man from Ukraine named "Kruschev." We could not, however, anticipate the consequences which were indigenous to one in a position of this kind in a totalitarian country.

Within a few days of the Russian occupation, part of our house was taken over once again, this time by Russian military officials who, some time later, were joined by their families. They seemed so insecure. The family of a lieutenant with a baby moved into my bedroom upstairs. One day my mother, hearing the young wife cough and sneeze, offered her aspirin. The woman looked at her and said, "Thank you, I do not want your pills. Everything is better in Russia. We have better aspirins—we invented the aspirin." That is how it continued. They were so unsure of themselves, and we felt superior; so no close ties developed. The Russian woman, never having been exposed to Western sartorial customs, would wear our nightgowns in the street. This would make us laugh, and that made them furious. They did not want to exhibit their complete ignorance of what we called civilization. We looked upon them as if they were Martians. The woman's silk stockings were thick and purple, the man's underwear red. They dressed in the most unfashionable way. They would outlandishly combine colors such as green and blue, an unthinkable combination, or in the summertime they would appear in the center of Lwow wearing deep cut dresses. To all our reproaches they would answer—those who answered at all—"And why not? Any color goes with any other color, and when it is hot, we can even wear cut out clothes in your town." They had no conception of fashion and that amazed us. They sewed all their own clothes, including brassieres and handkerchiefs, and they looked it. On Sundays husbands and wives would walk in the streets with their children, and they usually had three or four of them, a custom that in western Europe was not too prevalent. The affluent employed maids to take care of their children. The poor ones did not parade in the streets, or the men would walk alone while the wives stayed home with the children. The Russians assured us that they invented the telephone, the electric light and the automobile. Instead of pitying them, we would ridicule them. In my own rather provincial way I did not appreciate the deep cultural differences which existed between our countries.

This was the Stalinist period in Russia. Children in school, before their gym classes or any sports event, would shout, "Long live Stalin, the greatest sportsman in the world." He was also the greatest writer, artist, and excelled at everything, so they claimed. We were simply losing our minds. At times it seemed that we were surrounded by lunatics. The Russian youth honestly believed that in France, England, and certainly in Poland, the children were actually bitten by their teachers, and that their children were the only ones who were treated well in school. This is what they told us. What did they really think now that they had crossed their borders? This all happened in the years from 1939-41.

One day I was sitting in my father's room when a short Russian officer, who now occupied my parents' bedroom with his colleagues, looked in through the glass door from the foyer. He noticed me, smiled and walked in. This one has nerve, I thought. I was sorting some books from my father's library. He looked at them, then started a conversation. He liked the towns in Poland, he said. Then to my great surprise he added, "Your 'Pan' Marshal Pilsudski was a great man." For a Russian to say "Pan" was a major concession to the capitalistic world, and even to speak about Pilsudski was another. Even I, as negative minded about the Russians as I was, could sense it; and somehow I was ashamed for feeling so hostile. But only for a moment. Why did they come here at all, I wondered, and why in hell don't they go back to Russia?

Our boarders carried their guns when they went from their bedroom to the bathroom. Through the glass door my mother could see this, and she would always say, "Please, give me a sip of cognac. If I do not get it, I will faint." We all laughed, since my mother loved a sip of cognac even before the war, and she now looked for an easy way to get it, we thought. She placed the bottle at the side of the Gobelin chair which she once made, and which was now in the crowded room because with just two other rooms this was all that was left for us. But we were still laughing, we were still together, healthy, and that was all that mattered. Our sense of humor was still with us and kept us going. As a family we were closer now than ever before. My grandparents on both sides, my father's brothers with their families, my mother's three sisters, and my father's cousins were living in one town.

Slowly, the most difficult phase of the Russian occupation developed. In the deportations to Russia, the first to go were the known capitalists and politically prominent people. Many others from our little town left during the first days of resettlement. From our family were included the wife and children of my father's cousin who was an officer in the Polish army and now a prisoner of the Russians. Tereska and her two sons, Ernest and Stasio, were seized during the night. That was how the Russians operated. Tereska did not mind. She thought that she would be reunited with her husband. But years later, his name appeared on the list of those executed at Katyń—only historians of the future may be able to prove by whom, the Germans or the Russians.

In general, if one were not seized by surprise, it was not too difficult to evade Russian deportation. No members of the local population collaborated with the Russians. One need only spend the night across the street, to be spared. The police did not know the people, and no one was eager to make their task easy. If only they had behaved in the same way during the German occupation!

Our closest friends, the Schutzmans, were among the first to be rounded up, preceded only by the mayor and his family. Mr. Schutzman, one of the wealthiest oil well owners, had a most interesting library in his home. He collected old books. I saw a Koran there published 1,000 years ago. The Schutzmans also owned a refrigerator from the United States, the only one in town. In the summer we would use their swimming pool and play tennis on their home courts. They had two daughters and a younger son. The girls had attended a finishing school in Dresden before the war. The whole family was seized, including the grandfather. Interestingly enough, it was the old grandfather and one granddaughter who returned from Siberia after the war. All the others perished. The grandfather worked as a cow hand, and those who saw him on his return thought that he looked five years younger than he actually was.

It was my Uncle Lonek who left Boryslaw fearing deportation as a previous oil well owner. My Aunt Giza and Oles remained in a small apartment which was quite a distance from our house. Lonek's departure was a shock to our entire family, but it affected me but little. I went to the University of Lwow and as it happened, it was there that my uncle came to hide. We went to live with Aunt Zosia.

## Lwow: The Polytechnik

It was a gloomy day in October when my friends and I boarded a train to Lwow. We were all going to enroll in the University. We planned to study, and our enthusiasm was unbounded. We sat in an old freight train since all the newer trains had somehow disappeared. Before the war, the trip from Boryslaw to Lwow by train took four and a half hours, or via the "Luxtorpedo" electric train, only one and a half hours. Now after sitting in the train for two hours we were still in the station in Boryslaw. No one knew when we would start to move. But we really did not care. We giggled and planned our future. Two of my girl friends decided to study agronomy, I was hoping to become an architect; a number of the boys wanted to study electrical engineering. We envisioned the building of a whole new town. We felt quite capable. Our city would feature glass buildings with movable electric doors and beautiful flower gardens. And we would accomplish all of this by ourselves! The only one who did not intend to pursue a course of higher education was Nela. She was so lovely and feminine, and as her father correctly judged, best suited to become a wife and mother. We all wondered why one would choose such a prosaic alternative. For us, the future just had to be great—and for the time being, marriage was not a top priority.

I was not admitted to the Polytechnik until after I produced a statement signed by a local workers' representative attesting to the fact that my father worked for the good of the people and that the well being of the workers was always his greatest concern.

One year of studying gave me more than I really expected. I met some marvelous people and made lasting friendships in a very short time. It was not only the University atmosphere—which is always conducive to forming new attachments—but in our case it was the general political situation, the unstable times which drew people together. During the first year there were about fifteen women who enrolled for the architecture course, each quite brilliant. Generally, all departments included women except in the electrical engineering course where only one girl was registered. She was one of the most attractive girls in town and came from a prominent Jewish family in Lwow. Chemistry was predominantly a woman's study as was pharmacy. Women were also applying for medical courses in large numbers, but vacancies were few. Some chose veterinary school initially and then in the second year hoped to transfer to medicine.

I enjoyed every subject in my curriculum. I was most excited though by plane geometry, probably because it was taught by Prof. Bartel, the former Polish premier, who was a most fascinating lecturer. A year later he was among the first Poles to be executed by the Germans. As many as 600 people would gather in the auditorium to listen to his lectures, including many of his former students, who were now prominent engineers. He did not particularly enjoy the prospect of having women students in his audiences. Before the war hardly any were admitted to his classes, but conditions had changed now. He would often interrupt his lecture, and looking straight at a woman he would say, "This young lady is completely lost. I can see it in her eyes." Therefore we would all try to avoid sitting in the first few rows in his class. I was so enchanted with geometry that I decided to only marry a man who could determine where the line and the plane in space intersected. I never asked Tom if he knew.

Bartel addressed the Russian girls in class as "ladies," never "comrades." He was the only professor to do so. One of his students was the daughter of the highest ranking Russian general in command at Lwow. Bartel repeatedly addressed her as "Pani"—"Lady." We all had to suppress our laughter. The young girl was definitely very uncomfortable. We disliked her intensely. She barely acknowledged our existence. At the beginning of the school term we tried to be friendly. We told her that wearing floor length coats was not really haute couture. She looked at us rather cooly, and never after that managed a friendly smile.

The only close relationship with a Russian student my friends and I had was with Kola. He was a small boy who looked more like fifteen than eighteen years old. He would ask many questions; his eyes were alert, and he always smiled. Kola liked his life in Poland. He was fond of the way the girls dressed and the nicely furnished houses. We called him the "bourgeois" boy, something he definitely was not. The slightest criticism of the Russian system would cause his small face to exhibit a hardened expression. Yet he was the only one to whom we could get close. The Russians who were sent to Poland were probably trusted party members who behaved accordingly.

Lwow was overcrowded because of an influx of refugees from the German occupied zone and the Russian invaders or liberators. A certain number of square feet were alloted to each. Every apartment or home owner was ordered to accept tenants. Zosia was assigned a middle-aged Russian man, a civilian official, to whom we often spoke. He became fond of us and told us much about the Russians. We learned that you could never trust people, not even your own children. The little ones were encouraged, even in kindergarten, to report their parents' attitudes, to denounce them in order to keep Russia strong and to please her greatest hero, the mighty Stalin. He became their God. Thus was formed the thinking of the young.

When elections were held, barrels of caviar were brought into Lwow. Bread and caviar were free to the public and I could never eat too much of it. I was too young to vote, but it didn't matter since there was always only one candidate for each post.

At least once a week we attended school in the evening where we had to listen to propaganda. The talks would go on interminably. To keep us from leaving, the coat rooms remained locked until two o'clock in the morning. An obligatory subject was the history of the Party taught by the head of the Kiev NKVD. The required reading was not bad, and the second chapter, purportedly written by Stalin himself, read very well. We all wondered who really was the author. Still, we were unalterably opposed to the regime. We were told that once we completed our studies, we would be required to work for a few years in any place the government sent us. I wanted to specialize in town planning architecture. Because I realized that the monument type was beyond my ability to master, my place of employment would probably have been Siberia. I can still remember the reaction of my mother when she heard the news and my laughter at her horrified expression.

Unrest in the town was mounting. The difficult political situation also had its impact on our lives in the universities. The deportations to Russia were increasing. Many of the refugees from the territories seized by the Germans moved to the Russian sector of Poland but planned to go back to their home towns in the event the Germans lost the war. What wishful thinking! It was hardly realistic in 1940-41. Almost everyone registered to return to their pre-war addresses hoping that the right time would soon arrive. They never suspected that this alone could be used by the Russians as an excuse for their deportation.

One day, Fred, a friend of mine, was deported to Siberia with his father and younger brother. I had met him a few months earlier. One morning on my way to board the tramway (trolley car) for the Polytechnik, I realized that I had forgotten my handkerchief. I ran all the way back and when I returned, the 6:15 trolley had left. I was waiting impatiently for the next one when I noticed a young man, obviously a student judging from the books he was carrying. He was tall, slim, and what I noticed at once were his beautiful eyes. I always had a weakness for blue eyes, probably because my father's were this color. He boarded the same train and seated himself opposite me. The young man opened a book and read for the duration of the 25 minute ride. I noticed that it was an English edition of an Oscar Wilde work. I jumped off at the Polytechnik; it was already after seven. In accordance with the new rules, one could not attend a class after it started. My name was entered in a book kept by a school official in the hall. Just then my companion arrived. We stood there in front of the locked class door for an hour. This, of course, was distinctly not a disadvantage to getting acquainted. Fred was a chemistry student, a refugee from Silesia. I would not have thought much about, or taken our relationship so seriously had it not ended in the way that it did.

Fred was taken away by the police one night. I ran to the station with a thermos bottle containing tea and some food. There were many wagons there filled with people. The guard pushed me away when I attempted to get closer. I retreated onto the grass, but approached the train from the other direction. Then I noticed Fred. He was very pale, and looked very tired. He had already changed. Later the trains were sealed and only the faces of the people could be seen behind the bars on the windows. They were slowly being moved away from the station. They kept receding in the distance, and then they were gone. I was heartbroken. I cried for days remembering this scene and recalling the faces of the victims behind bars. I cried once more when a letter from Fred arrived describing the pitiful life of the refugees. People fought for food when packages from friends in Poland arrived.

Those who were ill did not get daily rations. In one of his last notes to me, Fred mentioned that two of his frozen toes might be amputated. I lived with those letters day and night. I could not determine where Fred and the others were, or why they were there. We were not aware of Stalin's methods. There soon came a time when I was not so sure whether it wasn't better to be in Siberia. But, by then, the letters stopped coming. Through all these events I stayed with my Aunt Zosia.

Under Russian occupation Zosia was forced to work. Families who did so received more privileges, and she did not have a husband. She was assigned to a bakery where she served as a cashier. In a way it was a choice job because she could buy as many loaves of bread as she wanted without having to stand in line for hours. Her job was very demanding. She started her chores at the bakery at six in the morning which meant that she had to rise at four. It was an hour before she arrived at her post. At the end of the day she was required to check and balance the cash receipts. If she was over or under by even just a few "kopiejeks", her Russian boss abused her by ranting and raving. But somehow she managed quite well. After her past life of luxury and leisure, she was now without a moment's rest with hundreds of people in seemingly endless lines descending upon her with their payments for bread. When I watched her making change, adding numbers in her head, in spite of the constant pressure of the crowd, I just could not understand how she could continue to do her job so ably. Through all of this she still managed to look quite beautiful and proud at her stand. She even learned the Russian language rather quickly and did all the calculating for the Russian customers in their native language. She was extremely capable in her own quiet and charming manner.

During the summer that the war started Zosia met an engineer while on her vacation in Krynica. He, too, was widowed, with two grown children. His daughter decided to study architecture one year before I did. Theirs was a very short courtship. There was so little time and no place for privacy. Her apartment was terribly crowded with the additional "boarders" assigned by the government. His situation was the same. And then the Germans invaded. He and his children were among the first to be sent to their death.

At home in Boryslaw the situation reached a crisis. After a year of occupation the Russians no longer needed my father. Their own men were by then well-trained to take over the oil industry in our region. They made strange accusations against my father. When fire engulfed two warehouses belonging to the oil company in towns east of ours, my father, as general manager, was held responsible for them. The main indictment against him was made at a meeting in front of all the workers; other charges included a denouncement of my father as a capitalist who owned the "Batia" Shoe Company in Czechoslovakia. This idea must have originated from the coincidence that the Batia shoe store in our town was located in the old Post Office building which belonged to my grandfather. Now it was incumbent upon my father to defend himself in accordance with the way in which the law was written. One could be accused of any crime. The accused was guilty until proven innocent and not the other way around. Czechoslovakia was sealed off from our part of Poland with no communication possible. It was all a contrived story concocted to get rid of my father. We also learned that one of the high ranking Russians wanted our house. We were told by a good friend that we should have been wiser sooner. In situations of this kind one should never occupy large houses. I came home from Lwow to be with my parents at this crucial time.

Now that my father was out of work, we received a notice to vacate our house in three days. This evacuation order was extended for two weeks. My mother tried to sell our crystal, china, silver and oriental rugs. Two women doctors from Moscow were among the potential buyers. When no one else was in the room, one of them came over to my mother and said, "You will get used to this life. It is not so bad. When we go to our room after work and sit at the table, we feel happy. You will get used to it." They were both Jewish.

The furniture and books were to remain in our house. There was no time to dispose of them. Then two workers, who had previously been employed by my father, went to the Russian town authorities and claimed that all the furniture in the house belonged to them as they had been exploited by the director. They were granted permission to remove our belongings. First they took the books, then all the furniture which they sent directly to the storage house saying that they would keep these things for us. In June of 1941 on the day the Russians left our town, the same two workers came back to my father and asked if he would like to have his furniture back. The workers of Boryslaw will always be heroes to me. What wonderful men they were!

Another Polish worker who heard that we had to move offered us his small house, which was a little out of town. We were very grateful. It had no running water, but at the street curb there was a well with a pump. The house was clean and pleasant. We were there for no more than two days when we were warned that during the coming night more deportations to Russia would take place, and that this time places on the train were reserved for us. We quickly left for the house of my uncle, the older brother of my father, who had the best background in the family. All his life he had been an upper echelon employee of the oil company, but never an owner or a top official. We spent two nights at his place and that was all that we needed. Again, none of the townspeople collaborated with the Russians. Not even those pre-war communists who by now were disillusioned with Stalin's system which proved to be not as utopian as they had expected. Also, the Russians never managed to bring out the worst in people as the Nazis later succeeded in doing.

My parents then insisted that I return to my studies in Lwow and they shortly moved to Drohobycz, a town eight miles away. My father got a job once again in an oil refinery and all his past seemed forgotten. Shortly before the Russians left, my father was summoned by the police and was kept there overnight, to the horrible chagrin of my mother. He was told that they had planned to deport him from Boryslaw, that he had no right to go to Drohobycz, and that they must now decide what to do with him. They mentioned that they would like to get some information from him regarding other people in the oil industry. He flatly refused. This was the last my father heard from them. Three weeks later the Germans invaded Russian-occupied Poland. How little we knew what lay in store for us. How naive and hopeful my parents had been. How very hopeful!

## Start of the German-Russian War

My classmates and I parted on Saturday, June 21, and made a date to go swimming on Sunday. We had just completed the measurements of a house in the old town of Lwow, one of our last projects in the architectural planning course at the Polytechnik for the spring semester of 1941. Alma, Niusia, I and a few boys decided to go swimming for the first time that season. With all our exams behind us, we felt relaxed and happy in spite of the Russian presence. I was especially elated since my A and B grades fulfilled the requirements for receiving the Stalin stipend for the fall semester. All my studying had paid off. I would be virtually independent for the next semester, or so I thought.

The next morning I arose leisurely and checked my swim suit, to see if it still fit after those long winter days in the library and eating cold, greasy meatballs (which I hated) or just Russian halvah in the student cafeteria. The muted sound of artillery shelling outside could be heard. My aunt and Walter were still asleep. I was the only one about except for Antosia who went to early Mass. Just then I heard her heavy steps hurrying in the foyer. She entered the room, looked horrified as I stood there in my swim suit, and screamed, "Are you crazy, miss, to stand there like that? The Germans are attacking Lwow." I smiled politely, thinking how incredibly foolish those peasant women were to believe the ridiculous gossip from their friends. "Antosia, Antosia," I said, pleased and still admiring myself in the mirror, "what silly ideas. These are only the usual army exercises."

But as I said that, with my mind already in the swimming pool, I heard the louder blasts of heavy detonations. Dear God, these could only be bombs, I thought. I must have dressed in a few seconds and so did Zosia and Walter, who were alerted by us. I ran into the street. Stunned groups of people were milling around, looking toward the sky or running in different directions with the most bewildered expressions on their faces, all talking or screaming to and at each other. "A bomb fell in the passage, Mikolaja," somebody shouted. I ran down the street toward the center of town. Trucks carrying Russian soldiers were moving slowly in a seemingly endless line. The faces of the men were somber, showing fear, and to a certain degree, hatred. They were tense and mistrustful of the local population, knowing that they were never liked here. They held their guns at alert, ready to shoot. I looked terrified, but even at this moment I almost felt sorry for them.

Then I suddenly saw Kola. I ran closer to his car and heard him loudly shout, "You all hated us so much. Now you will have the Germans here." I was aghast. It was true then. The Germans were approaching. The sound of falling bombs seemed closer now, and the first sirens started to wail. The Russians were completely unprepared as we all were. I quickly ran back to our house, catching a glimpse of people being carried on stretchers. In the basement of our home about fifty people were gathered, bewildered, and still not believing that all this was happening. As night fell, the noise abated for a while. Some men in our shelter assumed leadership and decided that we could return to our apartments. We moved swiftly, hungry and tired from the long confinement.

In less than an hour the planes were back. My sweet Aunt Zosia admonished us, "Before you go to the shelter, make your beds. Do not leave the rooms messy. What if we were killed and other people came here and saw the disorder?" It was just like Zosia. She straightened my slippers which I had thrown at the door and ran down terrified when the sound of a bomb seemed to be quite near. We stayed in the shelter for two days and nights with only short interruptions this time. During the second day the whole cellar shook and the noise was deafening. We all thought the bomb had fallen closer than ever. It did. It hit a hospital on the other side of the street. All the patients were killed in their rooms.

When we left the shelter, the Germans were already established in town, and there was no trace of the Soviets. Should we celebrate? What are we to expect from the Germans? How were my parents in Boryslaw and all my friends in other parts of town? I would never see my companions from the Polytechnik again, except for one or two, briefly, in the concentration camp. But on this day in late June I did not know that yet. How lucky we were that the horrible events which were to overtake us could not be envisioned or foreseen. Was it really fortuitous not to know?

# 3

·····

# Under German Occupation

## LWOW: SUMMER OF 1941

For the first few days after the Germans arrived we had no water or electricity. I told my Aunt Zosia that I would venture out since it was too dangerous to send Walter or Zosia. I was consumed with curiosity and wanted to go outside. With two pails in my hands I moved cautiously toward a small square where there was a water outlet. Quite a few others with containers were also coming from all directions. Suddenly the whole square was surrounded by SS or Gestapo men. Before we even realized what was happening, we were ordered to form a line and present our papers. The Aryans were dismissed. The Jews were told to march toward a partly destroyed building where the Germans had established their offices.

Next to me in line was a tall, beautiful girl named Alma. She had golden hair, deep black eyes and full lips. She was a first year veterinary student, as she informed me, and was trying desperately to leave our group by telling the German police that her mother was very ill and had to have water. All her explanations and pleading were of no avail.

We entered a partially bombed, enormous hall where we received our first introduction to German brutality. Crowds were already in the building. There was definitely no room to move, much less to work. We were told to put the dislodged bricks of the demolished wall to the side of the hall. I didn't have the slightest idea as to who the Germans were—SS or Gestapo—or whether it made any difference. Whoever they were, they were beating people wildly and brutally with whips. We had no inkling as to where the next blow would come from. In such a crowd we were unable to evade the falling whip.

Alma and I stood very close to each other, leaning against each other unbelievingly. An older SS man looked at us and said something which sounded like, "What a day, what a day." We answered, "Isn't it terrible in here?" or something to that effect, in perfect German. Neither Alma nor I knew Yiddish, and our perfect German seemed to surprise the man. Then, while the blows and screaming were taking place, he asked us, out of the clear blue sky, if we spoke French, as he did; he seemed anxious to show off his linguistic expertise. Once again we answered in fluent French, that we did. Alma added that she also conversant with English and I, with Italian. The man was delighted and started to lead us toward another part of the hall. He wanted to know who we were and what we could do. We had no idea of just what he had in mind. I answered that I knew how to draw plans and do lettering. Alma told him that she could do any kind of office work, though in fact she really could not. When she smiled so angelically she could convince almost anyone of anything.

Now we found out from him that they were all members of the Austrian Gestapo and that to avoid being caught again in another "Aktion" we needed an "Ausweise" (working card.) He walked into his office in the undamaged part of the building, typed out a paper for us and stamped it with the seal of the German eagle. This was all new to us, or we would have realized that he procured for us the best "Ausweise" in town, a most important document for anyone to have from now on. It stated that since we were employed, we were not to be assigned to any other job or to be seized by the police for beatings. The man then told us to report the next morning to work for him, putting signs on each door so that people would know where certain offices were located. We left the building, picked up some pails of water and ran home.

Seven thousand Jews were killed that day in Lwow at another

"Sammlung" place, we found out later. Alma and I bid each other goodbye, aware that we would see each other at eight the next morning. We did not know then, how closely intertwined our lives would become throughout the ensuing years. Alma is still a part of me.

### Janowska Camp: Mid-August 1941

The Viennese Gestapo was leaving. We were really sorry. Somehow, working for them gave us a sense of security. About ten Jews were employed there, women and men doing odd jobs, cleaning and washing clothes. I was still experimenting with some posters, which they planned to take with them, but subsequently forgot. It was here for the first time that I was faced with a question with which I would be confronted quite often in the future, at times from persons for whom I really cared, and thus it would hurt more deeply: "Are you really Jewish? You do not seem different from other girls." Dear God, I wanted to scream. Why am I supposed to be different because I was Jewish? What kind of worldwide racist propaganda was organized against us? It was as if they were saying you and your people are lepers, difficult to detect physically but deep inside you there must be something wrong, and certainly different. Do tell us what it is!

While we are also trying to cope with some of our more subtle problems, the situation in Lwow was becoming unbearable. Going to, and coming from work, we were forbidden to walk on sidewalks. Recognizable by our armbands we could be pushed around by any kid on the street, whether Ukrainian or Polish. Whenever we were near an SS man we hardly knew what to expect. We watched some Jewish men being kicked, pushed, pulled, or thrown in the mud. These were the "innocent" events, the so called harmless jokes which still made one's heart stop beating momentarily. Sometimes these little incidents of ridicule and degradation almost seemed worse than murder. And then a thought would distress me deeply, one upon which I hated to dwell: what was happening to my father and mother and all the others? I knew that they were alive and working, but this was not the only problem that worried me. Was somebody taunting them?

Shortly after the anniversary of Petlura—the great Ukrainian hero who murdered our people at will in his lifetime—was celebrated. This day was chosen for the most severe attacks against Jews. Thousands of them vanished from Lwow, among them my second cousin Artur, a nineteen year old student at the Polytechnik. His parents looked for him for months, but found no clue to his and the others' whereabouts. No one ever learned how they were killed.

The day before our Viennese employers left, they called us to the main office. The highest ranking officer of the Gestapo—I still could not identify him or his contingent—suggested that if we wished, he could get us jobs in a different work center instead of just "letting us loose" on the streets without working cards, which of course would leave us exposed to all manners of brutality. We eagerly agreed. He called a "friend," Obersturmführer Gebauer, of the German SS who operated a car repair shop for military vehicles on Janowska Street on the outskirts of Lwow, and asked if he would "employ" us. Janowska, then, a life style experience one could not imagine even in Purgatory, was graciously offered to us, and we accepted. We went there willingly many times. When I later recounted this to others, they would look at me in utter amazement. Did anyone ever go of their own volition to Dachau or Auschwitz to ask for a job?

We met in the morning and went in a group to Janowska. As we entered the courtyard we saw many of the SS: Obersturmführer Gebauer and Mohrwinkel, who was a friend and protege of Himmler. This was generally known. I took one look at them and I immediately knew that I had made a mistake. I felt terrified. They were standing in front of me, so tall in their greenish-blue uniforms, their granite-like faces unsmiling and expressionless. Do I really want to work here, I thought, but what choice did I have. They immediately decided how and where to assign us. Alma was immediately sent to clean their headquarters. Somehow, she was always the one people like to have around, looking, at times, too good to be true. I was placed in the main office to work in the reception room. I was soon to find out that this was where all the action was taking place. The others were ordered to storage rooms to sort tools and to clean. Alma and I lived in the same section of town, we came to work together and communicated constantly as the private quarters were adjacent to the offices. We ate together, compared notes, and informed each other about all the events that were taking place on both fronts.

Alma charmed everybody. Quite attractive in her cotton dresses, with bare shapely legs, starry eyes, and winning smile, she was admired by all.

I worked as an aide to Mrs. Nadel, a woman in her thirties who supervised the entire office staff. Later on, a secretary and an elderly Jewish man of German origin joined our group. Janowska camp was initially opened as a car repair shop where the actual mechanical work was done, in the beginning, by Polish mechanics. I was never that close to workers before, and now when they would come to the office for their pay, I was amazed to find out that they read newspapers and were politically well-oriented. Even in the most difficult situations I always appreciated these revelations and wished that I could share them with my father. At times, I thought if it were not for this war, I would never have discovered the variety of peoples that comprised our world. The Polish men worked here voluntarily, and their pay was good. All other tasks were performed by Jewish men forceably brought here every morning by the SS and Ukrainian policemen.

These groups were composed of young boys and men, pushed, beaten, and pulled as they were led through town. They would arrive at about eight in the morning and leave at five in the afternoon. It was August, the weather was warm, and once in camp the men would be assigned to the kind of work for which they were equipped. Most of them had no special ability and it was really an act of brutality to bring them here like a herd of cattle to be maltreated. In this way the bulk of those arriving each day were new and not knowing what to expect, were terrified.

The foremen in the workshop were usually the same Jews with special technical qualifications. As the transports arrived it was my job to record the men's names, their professions, and accordingly direct them to their foreman. This procedure became routine. Everyone knew that in a few hours the men would go home, and no one really cared what was accomplished. There were days, though, when Gebauer was in a bad mood and then beatings would start in the office during the registration. It was always amazing how the mood of the Obersturmfuehrer was immediately transferred to the Ukrainian policemen and other SS men almost as if they had been eagerly awaiting it. From the office the heart rending cries of those being beaten echoed throughout the yard. I would stand there in the office, trembling, but trying to look very

composed and just repeating—"Give me your name, please. It will
be better for you to be at work. Just tell me what you can do." The
men were so frightened that they could hardly talk. No one wanted
to divulge his real profession. It was generally thought that the
Germans did not like educated people. In Gebauer's case, it was
different. If he was in one of his more humane moods, he would
talk with lawyers or teachers and inquire about their previous ac-
complishments. If they spoke German fluently, he would assign
them to work in the office. In one room he even opened a sort of
craft shop for creative people. But everything was badly organized. The newly arrived people were in a state of terror, the
Ukrainian police were wild, and the rest of the SS men were idiots.
In this kind of atmosphere nothing could be achieved throughout
the day, especially since the whim of the boss was subject to
change, sometimes from hour to hour. It was all so senseless, so
completely hopeless. Still the beatings here seemed no worse then
those that took place in the streets.

In town everyone was talking about the ghetto that was being
planned for the Jews. Until then we were still living, my aunt,
Walter, and I, in the same apartment with Antosia who still helped
in the house. We knew that with the advent of the ghetto everything
would change.

As long as Alma and I were employed "securely" at Janowska,
we decided to take advantage of this situation and try get rooms
in the homes adjoining the workshops which belonged to Polish
working families. When we mentioned it to Gebauer—or rather
Alma did as I was always too scared to speak up—he offered to
send a truck for our furniture. Aunt Zosia as well as Alma's parents
felt that these belongings might be all that we could save during
the move to the ghetto.

Our room on Janowska Street was quite large with a kitchen
stove in the center. The entire apartment house had no indoor
plumbing; the only toilets were in small green outhouses. We lived
on the second floor. Below us was Mrs. Nadel, my boss, with
her husband who shared the same feeling that this was probably
the safest place in town. Shortly after, some of the foremen moved
there also. The Polish families near us, ordinary workers, were
kind to us. One of the women would cook piergo for us for thirty
zlotys which we could sometimes afford.

This was all happening in September when the weather was still warm. It was also at this time that I unexpectedly went to visit my parents. It seemed a miracle to all of us that as Jews we were allowed to travel. Kraut, the most colorful character in camp, arranged it all. He was a war prisoner brought to Janowska with two others from a war prisoners camp to help Gebauer organize the workshop. As a consequence he had much more freedom than the other Jews. One day he, the other two prisoners, together with two SS men were sent to Drohobycz by truck to bring back barrels of gasoline. They knew that my family lived there, and so they took me with them. We sat in the open truck, and the afternoon was beautiful.

We arrived in Drohobycz in the evening. They brought me straight to my parents' apartment. I entered and could not believe my eyes. My mother, a grandmother, and all my aunts were clad in silk dresses, the men wore suits, the candles on the table were lit—it was our Jewish New Year. We cried and kissed each other. I learned of the fate of many of my friends. Although I corresponded with my parents, so many things were left untold. A cousin of my father in a village near my town was stoned to death by Ukrainian peasants. The same thing happened to his two young sons, one about eighteen and his fifteen year old brother who ran to his aid. A similar tragedy befell the parents of my friend Lena. Her father, a Shell Company engineer, was taken from his house at night with his wife and stoned to death. My friend, then eighteen years old, and her younger sister were ordered to dress and join their parents, but were spared at the last moment. All members of our immediate family were still alive. At dawn Kraut came to pick me up and we left for Janowska. There was nothing better for me in my home town, no safer place to stay.

Things were happening quickly at this particular time. Situations would change hourly, but never for the better, although it was difficult to imagine worse events than the present ones.

The major change at Janowska occurred in mid-October, one which none of us foresaw, not even we who worked so closely with our bosses. One typical morning in October, as we crossed a field which lay between our apartment house and our offices, we noticed many more SS troops than usual, all running and yelling. Then, a much larger number of Jews was marched in by the Ukrainian police and the SS. These people were seized in the streets and included the usual Vorarbeiters voluntarily arriving now for their assigned daily jobs. Together there were about five hundred in a long line in front of the office. Names, and more names, and more frightened faces, some of them children who were no older than fifteen. By noon when the registration came to an end, the sound of an alarm resounded through the grounds. All workers were ordered to gather in the middle of the yard for an "Appel," and hundreds of Germans surrounded the entire area. Janowska became a concentration camp, and all the workers assembled there on this particular day were its first inmates.

We were stunned. There was not enough food for the people, no shelter, and no place to sleep, not enough water to drink, and no latrines. In our worst dreams we could not visualize a more harrowing situation. In October the weather was cool, windy, and wet. The SS men with the help of the Ukrainians encircled the entire camp with barbed wire. A lookout tower was erected equipped with powerful search lights. All these changes were completed within a few hours. Since Alma and I and the Nadels had our rooms on the premises—all the surrounding homes of the Poles were incorporated into the camp—the change for us was the least dramatic. Hundreds of others were forced to spend this first night outside on the ground, the luckier few inside the workshops on the floor. We took some of the office workers and some of the Vorarbeiters to our place, until as "preferred" workers they could find shelter in the adjoining Polish homes. No one slept that night. From the camp came the strident shouting of the guards and the screams of men being beaten. It was a terrible nightmare. The next morning word spread in Lwow that the Janowska work camp was changed into a concentration camp. Wives, mothers and sisters of men detained there on the previous day, appeared at the gate bringing clothing and food for their dear ones. The pitiful cries of the women who were not allowed to see the inmates behind the workshops, were shattering. We, the workers from the office, and a few of the foremen, were allowed to go to the gates to talk with those who were arriving. There was so little that we could say. However, we tried to comfort them by assuring them that all were alive. The SS men accepted parcels and divided them among the prisoners at their discretion.

Again, changes were taking place before our very eyes. After a day or two, the men who usually appeared decently clad, washed and well-groomed, even when forced to come here to work, were already beginning to look dirty, lost, and hungry. An amazing difference in these first days! And new unfortunates were being brought in, caught in the streets or delivered by the Judenrat. The mood of the SS was also drastically altered. With so many new policemen arriving here, trained in other concentration camps, hitting and shouting was constant. Barracks were being built, a kitchen was installed, but the need for immediate accommodations would not be fulfilled for weeks or maybe months. The prisoners deteriorated into a mass of dirty, ghost-like starving men. Each day the weather grew colder. Rain and mud all over made conditions intolerable. As we came to the office from our apartments in the morning we would see men lying on the ground swollen and half dead. In time, the SS men became wilder and meaner. They were all running now with whips in their hands, looking at the poor dirty souls as if they were creatures from another planet. All the sadism of the SS thugs now came to the fore. We saw human beings forced to undress, crouch and mercilessly be beaten with whips by the perverted SS men. To add to their travail food for the sufferers was becoming increasingly scarce. And the coldest winter in years was anticipated.

Alma and I brought pieces of ice-covered wood for our oven. It was useless. The water in a basin we tried to use for washing was frozen. In despair we broke chairs to use for firewood, also wood hangers and alas my books, my splendid collection on architecture that I brought here to save, were being torn apart page by page to start a fire. I still remember my feelings of disbelief when Alma and I did this vandalizing. Somehow, that brought the utter cruelty of the war closer to me. I was ripping apart art books which until then made me think that somehow, somewhere, we would survive; the world would be normal once again; and books and art would once again attain their exalted positions in the world of culture when the madness was over. It was childish on my part, but destroying my art books shocked me as much as did the sight of our beautiful spoiled dogs barking and scratching at the door of a butcher shop in Boryslaw begging for food. This happened when I went back there during the Soviet occupation after we had all left.

One cold winter evening the whole camp was on alert. A close friend of Himmler was coming to conduct an inspection. Gebauer and Movinkel were preparing a show for their guest, an evening of entertainment. We sat in the office not knowing what was in store. Then an "Appel" was ordered and the word spread. Some of the prisoners would be beaten in front of the guests— those who in one way or another disobeyed the rules this day. A young boy was selected, about 15 or 16 years old. All the lights were focused on him. He was placed in the middle of the yard and was savagely whipped. With every lash we heard him scream, "Mama." I sat at my desk plugging my ears with my hands but nothing could block out his piercing cries. I heard them for hours, I can still hear them today. The boy survived the beating. After a week, when he recovered, he became a favorite of the whole camp, even of Gebauer. He died of typhus a month later.

Later, Gebauer went to Germany for a few days. On the first morning after his return, he did not wear his usual SS uniform but a light blue jumpsuit. He knew that he looked well in it; we could see it in the expression on his face. For a while, he also seemed more relaxed and a little more human. But soon the same gray SS uniform and the old tenseness and cruelty reappeared.

One day during the winter months Mrs. Gebauer arrived. She was a tall blonde woman, heavy set, very quiet, even shy. From Alma, who still cleaned Gebauer's apartment, I learned that she was very polite. During her stay, of one week, life in the camp moved as routinely grim as always, but no extraordinary cruelties were committed. Just knowing that she was there, made me feel that we were being ruled by a complete royal court—a despotic king, a quiet queen, and all of us subject to their whims and aberrations. The juxtaposition of normal life—of a wife coming to visit her husband, or of a man showing off his new suit—with murders committed constantly by apparently "normal" people, made the situation so utterly incomprehensible, and most confusing. It was all so insane. People who seemed to be endowed with all the usual weaknesses were transformed into cruel beasts who seemed at times not to be human beings at all. I just could not understand it. No one probably could.

Just before the Janowska work camp became a concentration camp, a new typist sent by the Judenrat arrived. A refugee from German Silesia, she spoke German and Polish fluently. She was very attractive, in her mid-thirties, very sure of herself and not at all intimidated by Gebauer or the other members of the SS. Sometime later when the number of inmates increased, an additional part-time typist was once again sent by the Judenrat. She was a Viennese refugee, in her thirties, and looked very elegant in her pre-war dresses and the jewelry she wore. Gebauer definitely enjoyed having the two women in the office. His attitude towards them was very cordial and attentive. But at the same time his dual personality became more pronounced and obvious. In a split second he could be transformed from a human being into a ruthless Nazi warrior fighting on the battlefield of Janowska filled with the shadowy corpses of Jews. "Hurrah for the fatherland! Another emaciated Jew just fell." And that is how horrendously the days passed.

By the middle of winter, typhus was rampant in the camp. People were dying before our very eyes. Finally, Gebauer decided to call in doctors from outside who immediately evacuated the sick to the ghetto hospital. For a few it became a means of escape. Only there was no place to escape to. The Jews in the ghetto were being slaughtered by the thousands. A group of young boys made an arrangement with a Polish or Ukrainian driver to take them from the ghetto to the Polish partisans, who were hours away from Lwow. The man took the money delivered to him by the parents of the six boys, but took them directly to the Gestapo who rewarded him handsomely. All this was well known in the camp. A local Polish prostitute, Janka, who visited the SS men at Janowska periodically and brought a few of her friends for orgies, learned what was going on in Janowska and offered to help. She was a generous and humane soul in many ways and decided to hide a few Jews in her parents' apartment. Janka and her family were all shot, much to the despair of the camp's SS men. We all loved and respected her. From that day onward the word "prostitute" would have a new and enlightened meaning for me.

It was one of the coldest days of the winter. The inmates outside were moving like shadows, grimy, half frozen and starved. The scene was even more harrowing than Gebauer could stand. Suddenly he ran out of his office and ordered buckets of cold water to be placed in the middle of the yard. Then he randomly selected a few men and ordered them to undress. They were then forced to jump into the buckets of ice water and to scrub with brushes. The temperature outside was about fifteen degrees below zero. I was witnessing this scene through the window—it was one of madness, and sadism.

The lines in front of the latrines—plain wooden outhouses—were very long. The men in front, almost all suffering from diarrhea would scream, "Move faster," "Open the door." There was no paper in the entire camp, no toilet paper, no newspaper. Filled with rage and resentment we would, at times, take any paper from the desk in the office—any paper, except the lists of inmates, and we would give it to one or two of the men. But alas hundreds needed it.

Food was so scarce that finally it was only thing we could think of. In the morning I would eat my piece of black rubber-like bread and drink a cup of black coffee. Then I would sit at my desk dreaming of food until noon when we got a brackish, warm water containing a few unpeeled pieces of potato. In the evening our menu consisted of bread, some watery soup and coffee. I never thought that one could ever think of food only, all the time. I had fantasies during the night—I dreamed about rolls with butter, rolls with ham and rolls with jam.

The next day the procedure was the same. Long lines would form in front of pails containing food distributed by our cooks. We would pass in front of them with a dish, and they would pour the grayish looking dirty water into it together with a few pieces of rotten potatoes. If only I could have more of this water, I thought, and another piece of bread. I wished that I could stop thinking about it. But it was impossible. I would sit at the desk again and feel the same hunger pangs. That was the only yearning left in me.

Then there was the cold. It was unbearable in our room. We would come there at night and find ice in the basins, cups, and wherever we left some water. One night after starting a fire with frozen wood we went down to Mrs. Nadel, to stay there for a while until the room was a little warmer. Suddenly we heard screams coming from the front of our apartment house— Fire, Fire! The flaming wood in the stove dried sooner than we thought it would, and the curtains caught fire. We ran upstairs, opened the window to let the smoke escape and heard shouting from the tower—"We will shoot you—you are signalling the enemy." What enemy?, we wanted to ask. They were thousands of miles away. We poured water over the burning wood. The fire was extinguished, but now there was no way to rekindle it. It was getting colder by the minute. The acrid smell of smoke and the cold air was all that was left. We lay down in our clothes in one bed under all the covers we had. Again, we thought about what we would eat someday. I fell asleep dreaming about my rolls, over and over again. In my fantasy I could see the rolls that looked crisp, with shiny crusts, and pink slices of ham and other meats along with deep red jam. But I could not eat any of this even in my dreams. They were just there in front and all around me.

I had a cup of tea at Mrs. Nadel's one day. It was not real tea but something that only faintly resembled it, and Mrs. Nadel offered me a saccharine pill. The thought of saccharine excited me. I knew that it would sweeten the drink. I craved it so much that I put the tablet directly on my tongue hoping for a pure sweet taste. For days I could not forget my keen disappointment. It tasted terribly bitter and not at all what I had expected.

Life became a simple matter of satisfying our basic needs. All that we wished for was something to eat and to feel warm. Alma and I would awaken in the morning, half frozen, and compare our dreams about food. We were really not able to talk about anything else. During those very cold days we both developed the grippe. We ran high temperatures and were unable to get out of bed. All of our friends left to go to work not knowing that we were sick. We were alone in the apartment house, hungry and awfully cold. The coffee which was left from the previous evening was frozen and so was the water in our pitcher and basin. But fortunately we were together. We could talk to each other from our respective beds consolingly. We even talked about death. After all, we witnessed it daily.

Then, one of the worst camp SS men arrived, one who was on duty in the tower. He found out that we were absent or was sent by Gebauer to call on us. When he saw our condition he brought some wood, and lit a fire in our stove. He also brought and cooked a head of cabbage. That seemed like a miracle to us. This man who would whip or shoot people without compunction was sitting here telling us about his family, his wife and daughters. We could sense that he was enjoying himself talking about his home life, as if he had waited for this opportunity for some time. Two days later we were back at work, smiling up at him whenever we passed near the tower. We decided that at times even killers could be human, only the killing continued. The inmates did not have to be summarily liquidated any longer. They were dying like flies. The corpses were taken out to a sand mountain at the back of the camp. I had never seen those mounds, but I thought about them often. I could see pure golden grains of sand in my mind's eye. How peaceful it must be there, I thought.

By mid-winter not one of the original 500 men incarcerated on that fateful day in early October when Janowska became a death camp had survived. Only a handful of foremen who had seniority were still alive. As the new men arrived, it was my job to write down their names and ascertain their occupation clearly. These people were caught in Lwow and the smaller surrounding towns. They were terrified since this was the first procedure after their arrival at the camp. As before, I had to explain that Gebauer liked educated people, but the conventional wisdom was that they were persecuted more harshly than the others in the camp. For that reason none would admit to any high degree of intelligence or education. All my persuasion did not help; I was probably too terrified to behave in an encouraging way. Also, in this hell on earth there were no hard or fast rules. Every moment was different depending on the whim or mood of the almighty Gebauer and of a new man, a Volksdeutsche, sent in as an aide. He arrived with a dozen members of the Estonian SS whose enthusiasm for beatings was on a par with or even surpassed that of the Ukrainians. While they would brutalize a man it seemed that they were fulfilling one of their innermost cravings. I wondered what these men were made of—was this the real reason for establishing a death camp?

One day, a middle-aged man was brought in by a Ukrainian policeman. They caught him exchanging some foreign money in the street in Lwow. He was a writer from Austria. Just then Gebauer walked in. Intrigued by the money problem, he ordered the man to turn out his pockets and to place all his belongings on the desk. Some coins fell out together with a condom. Gebauer roared. "You verfluchte swine, you Jewish pig." He could be heard through all the offices. I did not know what infuriated him so. The other workers told me later this man was kicked and beaten until his face was completely smashed by Gebauer's boot. He was thrown out into the yard. I never did find out if he survived as I never entered his name on a card.

I had problems with the cards more than once. One morning we were missing a man, according to my list. We were checking and

rechecking them against the roll call ["Appell"] count on this particular day. Mrs. Nadel, the woman in charge of the office, myself,
and some of the "Vorarbeiters" were frantically trying to solve the
discrepancy in the count. Finally, the reason became apparent. I
had two cards for one man named Schneider. I spelled his name on
one, "Schneider", and on the other card, "Shneider". Why I registered him twice, or why he appeared in the office more than once,
I never could understand. But if in fact he did, I was fairly certain
that my spelling error caused the confusion. By then, Gebauer was
aware of our problem and it was up to me to explain the discrepancy to him. I entered his room with the cards in question in
my hand. Gebauer looked at one card then at the other, and finally
at me with his enigmatic expression. When he reacted this way, no
one could pssibly predict if he would strike out, kick, or shoot
someone. He did not utter a word, but returned to his paperwork. I
tiptoed to the adjacent office into the open arms of Mrs. Wachtel
and I started to vomit. I was sick throughout the day. One missing
man could have resulted in the death of five innocent beings.

It was New Years Day, January 1, 1942. The camp was very
quiet. Not one SS soldier was in sight except for those in the tower.
No Ukrainians were visible. Alma and I were walking slowly from
our room to the empty office. There was little to do. Two or three
inmates, with one of the prisoners of war, passed by. They appeared
to be slightly drunk. Where they got the whiskey, or whatever it
was that made them high, we did not know. We overheard their
discussion. They were talking about women. One of them spoke
about how much he missed them, and the others echoed his senti-
ments. I was amazed. In this hell to end all hells, one of the men
said that the worst thing for him was the lack of companionship of
a girl. "Oh, just give me a woman", I heard him say.

We quicly entered the office. I had never been in the presence
of such older men. I never heard this kind of talk, and I never
expected to hear it here, expressed by those oppressed and ter-
rorized people. That was a new insight on prison life about which I
never thought. All at once I became self conscious about being a
girl among all those men. It was a feeling that I never experienced
here before. I never heard this kind of talk again, and I never
wanted to. Those mere shadows of men looked nothing like
normal human beings I could think of as objects of normal

love. I was panicky, afraid that they would expect some reciprocal feeling from me, but all I felt toward them was great pity and horror which penetrated my entire body numbing me so as to make me incapable of any affection. Dear God, what were they doing to these men that even I could not look at them without a sense of horror? What kind of person will I become? What kind of person am I now?

A few days later I was standing in the office looking through the window watching some SS men beating a group of bewildered men who looked like ghosts risen from the grave. Gebauer, from his adjoining office, noticed my expression of revulsion. He was furious. I thought he would strike me, but he just screamed, "Do not look at those men. You do not have anything in common with them. I don't ever want to see you looking this way." Then he added, "You will never in your life be as well off as you are here." I stood there and said nothing. I hardly ever said a word to Gebauer and there was really nothing I could say now, but he went outside and the beatings seemed to subside. Every one of these sadistic beasts could, at times, exhibit some humane trait, if only briefly.

In those very bad days when hundreds of men were being brought in, I thought, among these unfortunates today could very well be my father, one of my uncles, or Walterek. God spared me that. No member of my family appeared while I was there. This happened much later. Yet, all the victims gathered there in the courtyard seemed an integral part of me.

A baby was born in the camp. The father was a foreman who lived with his wife in the previous Polish apartments not far from ours. He was a carpenter, well liked by Gebauer; his wife, who was just skin and bones, managed to carry the child through to birth. We all went to see the baby, even Gebauer. It was a tiny infant and it was almost unbelievable that a child could be born in a hell such as this. This event seemed to foretoken a better tomorrow. It was a miracle. God, will I ever have a baby of my own to care for, to love? But this hope and excitement lasted only for two days. The woman was ordered to leave the camp and to move to the ghetto with the baby. She decided to leave the child with her parents in the ghetto and chose to remain at Janowska with her husband. The same hopeless atmosphere became pervasive once again. I could not believe it—a mother abandoning her child! But it was to happen many times. The world did not seem a worthy place in which to live any longer. There was nothing at all to hold on to.

And then another event took place—one for which I was totally unprepared. The inmates learned that one of the cooks in the camp, himself a prisoner, was selling food. I never found out if the deal involved great amounts of the rations or just larger daily portions. Some of the men attacked the cook and found a great deal of money and jewels on his person. Gebauer was told this and he gave the inmates full authority to punish him as they saw fit. I felt sick and completely broken in spirit to think that one of our own men would take advantage of his position and sell the food that belonged to these half-starved people, to enrich themselves while so many were dying daily. A few hours later the culprit was brought to the middle of the yard and beaten mercilessly. I did not witness this scene. I hid in the farthest place in camp so that I should not see or hear the terrible things that were taking place. Later somebody told me that they took the cook back to the barrack and left him lying there. I'm sure that he died a few days later.

### The Italians

In mid-winter Alma discovered that on the other side of the camp, about a mile down the road, Italian military men moved in. There were many of them already in Poland. They were being sent to the Eastern front to fight the Russians. From their post across from the camp they sent cars for repair in our workshops. They were horrified at the conditions in Janowska.

Most of the men were college students, an artist attending the Fine Arts Academy of Florence, an engineering student from the Polytechnic of Rome and a number of law students. They started to come more often, bringing their cars for repair and just hoping for an opportunity to talk with us. My knowledge of the Italian language finally proved useful. They would offer us cigarettes and sweets. We were hopeful once again. There were still people who were humane, who felt and could cry for us, who would assure us that someday life would be normal once more. They even tried to convince us, in their short discussions, that people were basically good and what we were now experiencing was just a passing madness. They hated Mussolini and Hitler. We were quite drained by then, but the realization that there were still some normal people around even temporarily imbued us with a new strength and an awakened desire to survive. Until now we were surrounded only by the Germans, the Ukrainian police, the Estonians and the walking wraiths of inmates. Now something new had been added, people who arrived directly from Rome, Florence and Ravena, if cities like this were still in existence. Again, the usual question: are we really Jewish? They hardly knew any of our people in Italy, and now they were being fed all the Fascist anti-Semitic propaganda. What was there to answer? That we were Jewish but still human beings? We did not even have to tell them. I believe they understood.

This realization was all that was needed to bring us to our senses, to accept the fact that if we really wanted to survive we had to do something about it. We would repeat the words of those Italian soldiers, a good many of them miserable, pushed against their will into this country and the war, that somewhere life was still worth living. We were in such a state of apathy and despair that we held fast to their words as a sinking man would grasp for a straw. After being disillusioned with everything, a spark of hope was suddenly rekindled. We decided to depart from the camp.

I did not consider leaving Janowska before because I simply did not know where to go, nor did I care to go anywhere else. I believed that there were no alternatives. I could have been deported from the ghetto at any time to some other concentration camp, no one even knew where. The whole world seemed closed off. I did not even know if it still existed, if there was anything left besides this madness. But all at once, because of new found friendship with the Italians, my outlook had changed. If only I could find the courage and the strength, there might be a way out. All this new born hope resulted from meeting some kindly people. I could begin to think of myself as a woman again, not just a prisoner. It did not seem possible, but I realized that it would be easy to love again. When I decided to leave the camp, I was greatly influenced by the Italians, perhaps even infatuated with them. It was this good feeling that instilled in me the determination to fly in the face of the seeming impossible.

We left Janowska, Alma and I. We were never considered members of the inmate population. Women were not detained there yet; this happened much later. We also could not foresee how Gebauer would react when we told him that we wanted to leave. To our great surprise and relief, and to the complete disbelief of our friends, all he uttered were the words he used once before: "You will never have it as good as you had it here." This time we chose to find out for ourselves. We went straight into the ghetto.

As the gate closed behind me I wishfully hoped that the nightmare was behind me. Sadly it was not to be.

The conditions in which I found Aunt Zosia and Walter were heartbreaking. They were working on the outside and returned to the ghetto only for the night. Thousands of Jews from the ghetto had already been deported, the old, the sick and the children. Zosia in a flat, monotone voice told me a story of a little girl whom she cared for after her parents were "resettled." One night during more deportations, SS men and Jewish police entered Zosia's apartment and took the little girl from her dressed only in her nightgown. After an hour as Zosia and Walter were sitting there, shattered and crying, they heard tiny footsteps from behind the door and there was the young child. It seems that they had seized her too late. The trucks had left and the police sent her back only to take her a few weeks later in another deportation. There was very little about which I could talk with Zosia and Walter—only their horror stories and mine.

I contacted my parents who immediately started to make arrangements for my homecoming. As Jews were not allowed to travel, this was an extremely difficult task. An old friend of my father's, an Austrian by birth, was well-acquainted with a Viennese Gestapo man. He simply asked him if he could bring me from Lwow to Drohobycz on his next trip there. The man agreed, and kept his word. A few days later as I was sitting in our ghetto room, a member of the Gestapo entered. He was short, pleasant looking and wore a leather coat. He told me that he came to pick me up, and that I should get ready immediately. He allowed me to take my handbag only so as not to attract attention. I asked him if I should wear my Star of David armband. He hesitated for a minute, and suggested that I wear it under the sleeve of my coat. I could not even say goodbye to Zosia and Walter. I was never to see them again.

### Drohobycz: Spring of 1942

In Drohobycz my parents and our whole family, my grand-parents, my aunts and uncles and my cousin Elzunia and little Oleś were all living in the Jewish section now. The joy of seeing the entire family together was, at first, overwhelming. Everything seemed so unbelievably better here, but alas, only for the first few hours. The first night of my stay just happened to be the one when the "poor" Jews were "resettled" by the Gestapo with the full cooperation of the Judenrat. It was an unbelievable situation. I was sharing a bedroom with my parents. We had already retired in the brass beds that my sister and I slept in when we were very young. Then it all started. It must have been midnight. We heard the policemen running outside, and people screaming. My parents, however, told me they knew we would not be taken this night. It was not our turn, not yet. We lay there in the darkness, just listening and finally it all quieted down.

In the morning we found out how many hundreds were taken, but among them, fortunately, were no members of our family, friends or people we knew. The "poor" ones went quite willingly, without much resistance. They were told that they were being "resettled" in a better place where work was awaiting them. No one knew where they were sent, and no one ever heard from them again. Deep in our hearts we hoped that they were still alive. And this is how the "selections" were conducted thereafter. Certain people would leave and no one knew their destination. Those who were spared hoped to survive and prayed that their turn would never come.

For us, another day had started. My mother decided to present a gift of a large tablecloth and napkins to the wife of the Gestapo man who brought me from Lwow. My mother had ordered the tablecloth to be made of lace she brought from Burano, Italy. This man and his family were quartered in a beautiful villa which had belonged to a wealthy Jewish family before the war, friends of ours. All their furniture and oriental rugs were still in the house along with many additional valuables. The young Viennese wife was charming. She had given birth a few days earlier as did her mother who stayed with them. There was joy and laughter in the home, with maids and nursemaids busily running around in a different world just minutes from our Jewish section. The woman liked the tablecloth very much and was most gracious in accepting it, but it seemed that she really did not need it. Her nightgown and beautiful robe were made of silk and lace. She was still recuperating after her confinement. She knew her husband transported me from Lwow and she must have approved for reasons we could not guess. This kindness could have resulted in her husband's transfer to the Russian front. A terrible price to pay for a tablecloth.

I saw the man once again when I was working with a brigade assigned to digging the grounds to erect a foundation for a house. Passing in his car, he recognized me, slowed down and raised his hand in a fist. I could not understand what this gesture meant. Was it supposed to be a communist worker's sign identifying him as a party member, or just a simple acknowledgement to give me courage? I just smiled, not wishing to show my co-workers that I knew him. There were a few of them, nameless decent men, to whom all of us who survived owed our lives.

For the first few days I reported to the leaders of our Jewish community on how the camp of Janowska was organized. They wanted to know all the details. Here in Drohobycz, an engineer of agronomy was involved in organizing a number of productive workshops for Jews to enhance their capabilities for use by the Germans. He concentrated on the building of a farm with large vegetable gardens cultivated by Jews and on erecting villas for the German Gestapo who presumably were planning to spend many years here. As I was a student of architecture—many ages ago, it seemed to me—I was given a small group of six girls to measure out the foundation for a house from a plan given to me, and then to actually dig the foundation. After all the measuring was completed, I was told to supervise the digging only, and here I failed completely. Instead of overseeing the girls, I found that I was the only one who was digging all day long. I was not a leader—I could not give orders. One day a few details were working on one large field where more buildings were scheduled for construction. Behind us, an older man was supposed to be digging, but all he did was cough, with a shovel in his hand. The whole field extended across a villa where the head of the Gestapo in our town, Feliks

Landau, lived. We saw him come out on the balcony with his binoculars a few times to look at us. A great panic ensued. The old man, just a step away from me, was then shot dead from the balcony by Landau. Since this occurred late in the afternoon, we were dismissed. I could hardly walk home.

A few days later, because my superior noticed that I was a digger and not a supervisor, my job was changed. I was directed to a library where, under a supervisor who was an artist and a writer, Bruno Schulz, a group of people conversant with foreign languages was sorting out a Jesuits' library, brought here from a monastery by the German Gestapo. I remembered then that when I was about twelve years old and my sister spent so much time with her piano, I was, more than ever, drawing faces. The only good thing about my sketches was that I enjoyed doing them. I would spend hours in my room drawing continually. My parents finally suggested that I take private art lessons with a teacher from Drohobycz's Gymnasium—Bruno Schulz. Somehow that idea never materialized.

I shall always remember the face and penetrating eyes of Bruno Schulz. He was short, thin and fragile looking. His visage resembled those drawn by an expressionist painter. I remember now that he looked like the work of Heckel. He hardly spoke to the girls who worked there. He seemed very shy, quiet, and somewhat awkward. Once I noticed that he was sketching us. I looked at the drawing he made of me. Although I never had an exaggerated opinion about my looks, I was quite unpleasantly surprised. He drew my face and breasts only. Professor Schulz, as we addressed him, usually had a few of his friends present, a short man with reddish hair and a pretty blonde woman. Once I overheard them talking about Proust. I did so much want to tell them how much I admired that author, but, as usual, I did not have the courage.

I spent some very pleasant days in the library but only the hours spent there were pleasurable. Life in Drohobycz became unbearable.

It was on an otherwise uneventful day while I was at work that I learned that my father had been seized and sent to Lwow. When I returned home, my distraught mother told me that a search was made of our room and that my father was taken from his place of employment by the Gestapo for interrogation in Lwow. They also managed to appropriate a few pieces of jewelry which were not pinned to my mother's clothing. Someone reported that we had money abroad as well as valuables and cash at home.

I felt that this was the end. My father would never survive the interrogations. We tried to utilize all possible channels for help. We called Zosia in Lwow who approached everyone there who knew my father. A rumor was rife that for a few thousand zlotys (about 10,000) my father could be freed. The money was collected by Zosia from friends who did not hesitate to contribute, knowing full well that we would send the funds back from Drohobycz somehow. Also, my mother called Römer, my father's German boss, who succeeded my father as administrator of the oil industry. The man immediately left for Lwow. In a few hours he secured my father's release, and the jewelry was returned. Meanwhile, the money was paid by my aunt. Both interventions evidently helped. My mother gave Römer a black pearl pendant in a platinum setting attached to a long platinum chain. We could see that he liked it, and he insisted on paying for it. My mother, of course, maintained that this was only a small token of our appreciation.

My father was unharmed. He had been interrogated in a prison about money he was supposed to have secreted in America. Before being taken to prison he passed through Janowska. He had never realized where I was before. God spared me from seeing him there even while he was in transit.

A big resettlement was imminent. We could almost feel it in the air. The situation was increasingly tense. No one felt safe any longer. The "poor" ones had already been taken as well as those without jobs, qualifications or the ability to work. During one of the minor deportations when only the old and those unable to work were rounded up, we hid my grandparents in a double closet. We sat on the floor near the window in the dark room to avoid attracting attention; and, terrified, we watched the activities in the street. It was a wild night. People were screaming, dogs barked, and the drunken SS men were singing. We saw them enter our apartment house. We sat down quickly at the table. Each of us tried to look busy. My father opened the door, two SS men walked in, inspected our papers, looked around the room, and walked out. My grandfather, who was praying in the closet—lately it was his sole activity—did not even hear them. My grandmother did. When we let them out of the closet she almost fainted.

## Malkale

After one of the deportations, while I was still in Drohobycz, a little girl was found in a deserted home. People would be assigned to take care of orphaned children. In this case the girl was sent to my mother for a meal. She was about three or four years old. Once she was shown where our apartment was, she would come by herself and stand by the door without uttering a word. We tried our best to make her feel comfortable and more at ease. We smiled and attempted to talk with her, but nothing could change her serious demeanor. Her hair was reddish blond and curly with brown eyes and a very pale complexion. After a few days she told us that her name was "Malkale." Now at least we could address her properly. One day my mother found a small rag doll. We were quite anxious to give it to the child. When Malkale came and sat down at the little table we had set for her, my mother showed her the doll. Her face lit up immediately. She started to talk. Words flowed from her tiny mouth. I could not understand her at first, but I soon became aware that she was speaking Yiddish. The child obviously could not speak Polish. She smiled and talked to us and to the doll. She clutched the doll to her little body when she left. After one of the other deportations she did not return. We sat there, my mother weeping and we just looked at each other. Malkale will always have a special place in my heart—right there with my own children. There never seemed to be enough time to cry for those who were gone.

Now the day of the big deportation arrived. My father received permission to bring his immediate family to stay for the night at the offices of a German director of the oil refinery where my father was also employed. We decided to take Oleś with us since he was recuperating from the measles and an ear infection. All other members of our family made arrangements for other hiding places. We left at sundown, my father, mother, little Oleś and myself. Aunt Giza, Oleś's mother, hugged him at the door and with a voice choking with tears said, "Perhaps you are saving his life by taking him with you. We may not be here when you return."

It was a pleasant summer evening. All of our attention was concentrated on Oleś, still weak from his illness, but so brave and independent. He just had to walk in front of us wearing his navy blue beret and a neat little suit with a white shirt and a tie. It took about an hour to reach the offices which would be our hiding place. We entered the building and went straight to my father's room. It was getting quite dark. We put Oleś to sleep in an arm-chair, and the three of us, with pounding hearts, sat near the window. At about nine or ten o'clock we heard noises coming from the street. As usual, before an "Aktion", the SS men were getting drunk. Some admitted privately that they could not do their job as well when they were sober. Some even said that they could not do it at all when they were not drunk. From our po-sition we could see the SS men running with their dogs, shouting, laughing and talking. They pulled Jews out from their shelters, led them to the streets and threw them into waiting trucks. The beatings, the screaming, and the barking of dogs lasted for hours as the three of us sat on the floor in the dark room, terrified, thinking only about all of our dear ones in other places. Were they safe, or were they too being subjected to the bestial indignities of the SS? It was late at night when the last trucks crowded with the deported left the streets. Only the obscene laughter of the SS men could still be heard. We left our hiding place early in the morning and moved toward the Jewish section. We experienced the terrible feeling of anguish—who would still be there?

What a feeling of gratefulness and relief! Once again our happi-ness was short lived. My grandparents in Boryslaw, my father's parents, and my Uncle Joseph's wife and daughter, my little thirteen-year old cousin Zosia, all had perished. Joseph, Fanny and Zosia stayed at home during the "selection" relying on my uncle's valid working papers to save them. They had put my grandparents into a specially prepared hiding place at the back of the house. When the Gestapo came they immediately took my aunt and Zosienka, allowing only my Uncle Joseph to remain. He objected and accompanied his wife and daughter. After they left my terrified grandparents came out of hiding only to discover that all their children had been deported. Soon another group of SS men rushed into their house, found them in the room and took them also. My grandfather was pulled to the train by his beard because he was partially paralyzed and could not walk. There he met my uncle and his family. They were all in a wagon en route to Belzec where all Jews from our region were to be executed. But at the last moment an SS soldier once again pulled my uncle from the train claiming that he was too valuable a worker in the oil industry to go to his death now. The train left without him, and it was from him that we later learned all the details.

I did not see my father cry when he found out about the death of his parents. But for the rest of my stay in Drohobycz I saw that he was awake every night. He could not close his eyes without seeing a vision of his mother. He said this only once: What was my grandmother thinking when the Gestapo took her? Was she wondering where her three sons were and whether they would be able to help her? I could feel that his heart was breaking from the agonizing pain, but I never saw a tear in his eyes. The deportation in Boryslaw was conducted by the Gestapo from Lwow and was personally supervised by Gebauer.

This particular "selection" left the Jewish people divided and bitter. Many unpredictable situations arose. Some families who paid Poles or Ukrainians for hiding places did not want to allow Jews who did not pay into their hiding places. The spaces were usually rather small, making crowds too difficult to control. Complete silence, even holding one's breath for a while was, at times, necessary.

A young girl in Boryslaw was not permitted into an elaborate hiding place prepared by the Judenrat for their families. When she was caught by the Gestapo she led them right to this place, and all the wives and children of the Judenrat members were deported. They all died. After this "Aktion" a different mood prevailed. Anyone who did not look truly Semitic, especially among the young and the courageous, was encouraged to leave the ghetto. Aryan papers were being bought from Poles or Ukrainians or received at times from friendly priests or nuns.

After long discussions with my parents I decided to try to escape. We were too proud to ask a priest for a birth certificate, and we would not approach any Poles to buy one. My father learned that there was a group of Jewish chemists who forged papers for only 250 zlotys, just enough to cover their expenses. They told me to select a name and I chose that of the daughter of our cook— Krystyna Kozlowska. They then prepared a falsified "copy" of my "original" birth certificate, and in my real papers, as in my Russian passport, they chemically erased my real name and wrote in the new one. They also changed my nationality from "Jewish" to "Polish." It was done quite well, but if anyone carefully scrutinized my passport, the erasures would be easily discovered. Interestingly enough, the chemists did not succeed in erasing my name on my old Polish passport. The original color of the paper on which the chemical was used changed into a deep pink and I could therefore never use it. The most crucial matter was obtaining working papers from an existing office in the event that a future employer required references or wished to check one's identity. To obtain these documents my father approached a Ukrainian engineer, who previously worked in the company my father had administered, and who now held an executive position with another firm. The man agreed most graciously although it could have cost him his life. He wrote out an affidavit for me. As he gave it to my father, he added that he hoped, in the not too distant future, to visit my father in this same office where they could reminisce about their past difficult times. If only there were more people like him, many more of us would have survived. This marvelous Ukrainian was not a close friend of ours before the war, yet he was willing to risk so much for us. We did not ask our friends, not wishing to embarrass or put them on the spot. Not one of them volunteered. It was only much later that help was offered to my parents, again by almost total strangers.

Now I had to learn Christian prayers, as it was the practice of the police and the "denunciator" to order people they suspected to kneel in the street and recite the catechism. I was young. My memory was excellent. I soon was able to master the few important prayers quickly.

I was supposed to leave town with Gala, a friend of my parents, a young woman who was about ten years my senior. She intended to leave for Krakow which pleased me, as Alma was already there with her Aryan papers. At the last minute my plans changed because my papers were not completed. But Gala, not wishing to postpone her trip, left without me. She assumed a Ukrainian identity since her black hair and blue eyes made her appear more Ukrainian than Polish. She traveled dressed as a widow in deep mourning with a veil over her face to avoid recognition by local Ukrainians when she left town. She did not get far. At a few stations past our town, German police started checking the papers of all train passengers and asked her a question which she thought she answered in German, not realizing that she was substituting

Yiddish for German. She was arrested on the spot and eventually executed. I did not find out about this sad event until much later.

After two days my papers were all in order, but since I was travelling alone, I decided, on the spur of the moment, to go to Lwow instead of to Krakow. I did not know Krakow at all and feared that I would have to ask too many questions to become oriented. In Lwow I knew my way around in spite of the fact that I was not a native, so I assumed I would be fairly safe. Also, the Italians were still stationed there. On the evening before I left I lightened my hair with peroxide. My aunts and my mother felt that my reddish-blonde tresses were atypical for a Polish girl. We decided that I should wear my navy blue suit with a white blouse and red earrings. I was to hold my navy blue felt hat in my hand and carry a small suitcase containing only my essential clothing. The rest of my apparel would later be sent to me by my parents. I would wear my Star of David armband while passing through the few streets near our house, then I was to discard it.

The first train for Lwow left at seven a.m. As the station was about one hour's walk away, I left the house at five in the morning. When I turned around a few steps away from the house, I saw both of my parents standing at the door crying. That was the first time in my life that I saw my father cry. He blessed me before I left. This also was a first for me. It felt so good.

I walked through the deserted streets to the railroad station located a little out of town. The October morning air was clear and pleasant. I breathed deeply to quiet my pounding heartbeat. When I arrived at the station, I learned that the morning train was cancelled on this particular day and that the next train was scheduled to leave at eleven o'clock. I quickly decided that waiting at the station would be dangerous for me, so I walked over to a small peasant house on the side of a field. A child was playing outside. I asked a pleasant looking young woman nearby if I could sit on her porch to wait for the train. She readily agreed which was most reassuring. I probably looked like an Aryan to her. A few hours later I was on the train. I was almost certain that a woman who sat near me, and who stared constantly at me, was a former maid of one of my relatives or friends. If she recognized me she never let it be known, or, as I assumed then, she was not positive enough to make an accusation. She just stared at me as if trying hard to remember where she had seen me before. Again, much later, I heard that a few days after I left, two girls who I knew from Gymnasium, and who were a year younger than I, attempted to escape in the same way that I did. Unfortunately, they met two Ukrainian policemen along the way who recognized them. Both girls were shot in town on that very day by the Gestapo to discourage further similar attempts.

### Lwow Again: October 1942

My train was delayed at every station. I arrived in Lwow in the evening and not during the day as I had anticipated. To my great surprise there were Polish people at the station offering rooms or beds for rent for the night. I hurriedly followed a slightly drunken older man to his house, just to get out of the station crowded with Ukrainian and German police. In his apartment his wife had prepared a clean bed for anticipated lodgers. We were all to share the same room, the husband and wife and their three children in one bed. I lay there listening to the snoring man, to an occasional outcry of the children, and thinking about all the others in Drohobycz. I was too tired to plan for tomorrow. Another chapter in my life had begun, the most difficult one of all. But I did not know it, not then.

On the next morning I left my suitcase in my room and went into town. I was walking through the streets of Lwow nicely dressed, but without my armband. I was not scared, just very excited. It was a beautiful day. I hoped for the best. First I went to the post office to send a telegram to my parents using the prearranged code to let them know that I had arrived safely. Then things began to happen almost by themselves. The first person I met after leaving the post office was a neighbor of ours from Drohobycz, an attractive blonde Jewess who came to Lwow with her husband. For security reasons they were planning their lives separately. We decided to look for a permanent lodging for the both of us. For the time being she would share my bed in the room near the station. We were both relieved not to be alone. Two days later we found a room through an ad in the paper, near Kulparkow in Grochowska Street on the outskirts of town. Our landlady, an old maid and the daughter of a mailman, greeted us warmly. We were to share her bedroom. She had a large extra bed we could use until her lover, a German Wehr-macht soldier, could return to Lwow. We could then sleep, for a few nights, on the kitchen floor until his departure. What could be cozier or safer? I then contacted my parents who sent all my clothes to my new address.

We were both looking for a job. My friend found one as a live-in governess to a German child. I found employment as a cleaning girl for military generals who commanded the prisoners of war camps. The ad read: young "intelligent" girl needed for cleaning military apartments. One hundred twenty girls applied for the job but I was chosen. My fluent German helped, but then of course no "intelligent" Polish girls would apply for this kind of work, so it was rather easy for me to win. It was a matter of life and death to have this job as I needed the marvelous Wehrmacht worker's "Ausweise" which came with it. Now I could probably get a Kennkarte in Lwow, pointing out that I had a good job as the reason for coming here to live. I went straight to the town offices, which were crowded with German Gestapo, Ukrainian police and Polish workers. My passport with all the erasures was examined by two members of the Gestapo. No one questioned it. I succeeded—I had my Kennkarte. If I only could have called my parents!

The man I worked for was an old German aristocrat, a general who was placed here in a bureaucratic job as head of the Polish war prisoners' camps. He was assigned one soldier who arrived early in the morning to polish his boots and a chauffeur who picked him up at eight o'clock. The general did not return until late in the evening when I had already gone. During the hour from 7 to 8 in the morning I would help his attendant prepare breakfast. Then the general would let me know if he wanted some special cleaning or washing done for the day. After his departure, I was on my own until five p.m. when I would leave for home. It really seemed unbelievable.

I wrote a letter to my parents and sent it to the address of a Polish co-worker of my father's. I wanted to share my good fortune with them. Then I wrote to Alma in Krakow to inform her about my whereabouts. A few days later she arrived at the general's apartment. We talked for quite a while. It was dangerous for her to come to Lwow, her native town, particularly because she was very pretty and always attracted attention. But that was Alma, so sure of herself—too sure as events later proved—but at the time we just did not think about it. We were together for two whole days, and then she left for Krakow.

As the days passed the initial excitement of living outside of the ghetto abated, and I became more tense. People in the building in which I lived asked my why I came to Lwow. My landlady, however, preoccupied as she was with her thoughts about her lover, did not bother me. Occasionally I would meet people in the streets who gave me long questioning looks. One day I was waiting for a friend when a young Pole approached me and said, "Don't stand here, move quickly. You are being observed, you are Jewish." "Of course not," I shot back, but I was not sure if he was trying to find out or if he was really concerned. I was also suspicious of a woman who cleaned the upstairs apartment in the Wehrmacht establishment. She told me that she was the wife of a Polish officer, a prisoner of war. One day she watched me closely while I was ironing one of the general's shirts. She could tell that I had never done this before. She showed me how to fold it, but she gave me a questioning look which made me quiver. A few days later I met another "cleaning lady" from our building who said casually, "Oh, you know the police were here yesterday. The wife of the Polish officer upstairs was Jewish and some one recognized her and denounced her." I almost collapsed. So the woman I was so afraid of might have sensed that I was Jewish and wanted to talk with me. I was blind not to recognize it.

Somehow life was becoming complicated again. I had to be on my guard constantly. I did not know who my friends or enemies were. There were also new registrations for something or other. I was always required to show my papers and face those questioning eyes of the SS men, or even worse, of Polish workers or Ukrainians. They could recognize a Jew more easily.

One day, on the way to my job I met a group of Jewish men who were being led to work by German SS and Ukrainians. I watched them, unable to move. They also looked at me and I was sure they knew that I was Jewish. I wanted to touch them, to go with them— but I was just stood there transfixed, terrified, and miserable. On another morning I saw a young woman with a baby in her arms being pushed by a Ukrainian policeman. She pleaded, "Let me go, I am not Jewish." My heart stopped beating. I knew that she was

Jewish. I could imagine what was going to happen to her, and I could not help.

I tried to contact Zosia and Walter. I received a note from them through my parents asking me to meet Walter in the building where he worked outside the ghetto. I went there. As I was climbing the stairs in the dark, someone grabbed my arm and tried to stop or seize me. I did not know if I was followed or if I was set up. I ran out and never came back. I have not seen Walter since, but I have thought about him and Zosia every day.

It was on a cold day in early December when I returned to my apartment. There was my mother sitting with the landlady, Stasia. I almost fainted, but I could not ask any questions. My mother, I noticed immediately, had attempted to make herself appear Aryan. She wore a bright colored blouse, colorful earrings and attractive lipstick. To my great surprise, she really did not look Jewish. Her coat, which she threw on the chair, was light gray with a fur collar. Jews were forbidden to wear furs since the German occupation. We kissed casually, happily, as if it were not unusual for my mother to visit. We joked and spoke about trivial matters until we were alone. Then I learned that the situation in Drohobycz was critical and that my father had insisted that my mother leave immediately. There was no time to notify me. My mother's adopted new name was Judwiga Kozlowska. She had working papers provided by the same wonderful Ukrainian who supplied them to me. My mother slept with me. Just then our landlady's German lover arrived. We moved to the kitchen and to Stasia's surprise, we did not mind at all. Everything was fine. The lover left after two days, but I sensed that Stasia could not understand why my mother stayed in such an awkward and embarrassing situation. We tried to explain that she was here visiting friends. But I still felt that Stasia was doubtful in the least.

One night when all three of us were already in bed, we heard a knock at the door. A Ukrainian and Jewish policemen were there. As they entered the room I threw the covers over my mother's head and jumped out of bed, standing there in front of them in my silk nightgown. I trembled so while I showed them my passport and I kept repeating, "I am so cold, I am so cold." The two policemen examined my passport. They glanced at my bed where my mother's black hair showed from under the covers. But they left. I went back to bed and Stasia asked, in astonishment, why I hid my mother. I explained it was because she did not as yet have a visiting permit to stay in Lwow. During the rest of the night I was barely able to regain my composure. I was also afraid that my mother might collapse. The worst problem was that we were unable to say a word to each other because of Stasia's constant presence. We learned what caused the search much later. The husband of my first roommate, Lusia, had been caught by the Gestapo. When beaten, he revealed the previous address of his wife. The police were therefore looking for her and not me. It was a miracle that they did not subject me to interrogation.

On the next day my mother decided to leave. She went to her brother, Ludwik, then head of the Radom Judenrat, who tried desperately to accommodate her in the Radom ghetto; but my mother did not feel any safer there and returned to Lwow. Once again, she was placed by a previous employee of my father's with a Polish family. But that seemed too dangerous for all concerned. Finally, as she did not know what to do anymore, she approached the German director of the oil industry, Römer, who lived in Lwow but was in close contact with my father in Drohobycz. He had once helped my father out of danger and was now ready to assist my mother. He told her to come to his place immediately and arranged for her to live there as his housekeeper. He had a Polish girl friend until his wife arrived from Frankfurt. Both women treated my mother marvelously, and she never knew if he told them the truth about her identity. Römer proved himself to be a most understanding anti-Nazi. He treated my mother as if she were a welcome guest. While he was in Drohobycz he would report to my father on how she was faring.

My mother's major problem was the superintendent in the building, an elderly Ukrainian woman, who somehow sensed that something was wrong. My mother slept in a narrow bed in the alcove of the kitchen and hardly ever went out so as to avoid meeting the superintendent or others. I wondered how long she could endure this life in addition to the constant worry about her family. I was really afraid that she would collapse.

One day Lusia, my first roommate, returned. She had lost her job as a governess. With her husband in prison, she felt sick and desperate. Once again she moved in with me. We hid the whole tragic situation from Stasia. Lusia felt worse with the passing of each day, and her sickness was not just despair. It was dangerous to call a doctor, but we could not manage any longer. Stasia could not understand why we did not call one. Finally we asked her to call the doctor she used. He diagnosed her illness as typhus and took her to a hospital in an ambulance. I saw her only once more when she came to ask me for some clothes after she left the hospital. Her blonde hair was shaved down to her scalp, she was woefully thin and could hardly move. Without her blonde hair her Aryan looks were seriously diminished. She decided to move into the Lwow ghetto. That was the last I heard of her.

My life was also becoming increasingly difficult. I knew that Lusia's husband was still in prison in Lwow. The very thought of his being interrogated by the police was a nightmare. I felt that sooner or later he would divulge my name as another Jew who was in hiding with forged Aryan papers. I did not feel safe in my place but did not have the energy to act. When I was at Janowska it seemed that even one step away from camp would bring me closer to freedom. Now that prospect seemed so far away and realistically out of reach. At Janowska I was with friends, and in Drohobycz I had my family. Here I was so forelornly alone. Then I learned that our Italian friends had probably been killed near Stalingrad. Everything seemed so dark and hopeless, and there was no one to whom I could turn. I felt extremely tired and helpless.

At this time the general for whom I worked was away and was not expected back until late night. While cleaning his apartment, I got the feeling that it was not worth the strenuous struggle to survive. I opened the gas jet in the kitchen and began to inhale. I must have lost consciousness. Then I heard voices. I thought that I had died and that my sister was near me, talking and singing. The voices became more voluble and harsh. I opened my eyes. There was the general, a German doctor and a few other Germans. The general came home sooner than expected and thus saved my life. Everyone inquired why I tried to commit suicide. I told them it was because my fiance had left me. That sounded like a good reason to them. When the others left I told the general that I was Jewish. I did not want to fight for my life any longer. It did not seem so important. He was stunned.

He really was at a loss for words. When I left his apartment I still felt sick. My head hurt terribly. I stopped at my mother's. I did not tell her what had transpired, but I did complain of a severe headache. After a few hours I left since her "boss" was expected back. We did not wish to confront him with a mother and daughter.

The next day when I came to work, my general, with a very sad expression on his face, told me that I could no longer work for him. If it was disclosed that he knew I was Jewish, he risked the strong possibility that he would be sent to the Russian front as old as he was. At any rate, that was the reason he gave me for my dismissal. He presented me with all his food stamps and his best wishes. He was a decent man who did not denounce me and even agreed to hire a Ukrainian girl I knew to clean his apartment. The young lady I suggested worked in an Italian hospital at Kulparkow on the outskirts of Lwow and wanted very much to work in town for the German Wehrmacht. I called her and she enthusiastically accepted the job and offered to recommend me to her Italian employers at the hospital. On the next day we switched jobs.

I was to meet the general once more a few days later when I discovered that I had left my high tied shoes at his apartment. I went there expecting to meet the new cleaning girl, but only the general was in. He really beamed when he saw me. He told me that he could not stop feeling guilty for not helping me. He could not sleep nights thinking about my situation and his inability to ameliorate it. But my shoes were not there.

I then went to the Ukrainian girl's apartment to ask for my shoes. I could not endure the winter without them, and I could never replace them. They were the ones I wore in high school, and the best I owned. The girl's policeman boy friend opened the door. When I told him why I came he screamed, warned me not to show my face there again, and slammed the door. Terrified, I departed. That was the end of the search for my shoes. I somehow managed without them. Only later did I find out that the young lady and her friend knew that I was Jewish. He could have taken me directly to the police station, but he chose not to. I would always be grateful.

Kulparkow was a hospital for the insane part of which was occupied by the Italians wounded from the Russian front. One day I was walking with two other girls, and we entered the insane asylum by mistake. A few women were lying in beds. When we walked in, they sat up. One of them, looking directly at me, screamed, "And what are you doing here?" I was sure that she knew that I was Jewish and that I was hiding here. I ran out of the building. My heart was pounding. I just hoped that my companions did not know how scared I really was.

My work at the hospital consisted mostly of peeling potatoes with the nuns who ran the institution and with some Polish girls and Russian refugees. I would often serve as translator for the Italian head nurses, some of them countesses, who were not able to communicate with the local help. For a diversion I would sculpt small figurines from the potatoes. Everyone seemed to like them.

It was to this hospital that all the Italian soldier casualties were sent from the Russian front during the winter of 1942-3. Their feet were so frozen that their toes came off with their boots. I did not see this as I was in the kitchen peeling potatoes. The nuns would tell us these grim stories.

Easter came, and the nuns and the Polish girls sang and prayed for hours on end while peeling potatoes. I never learned those Easter prayers. I worried if they wondered why I did not participate. As I sat there my thoughts wandered from my own situation to that of my family's. How could I bring Walter here? How could he leave for Italy with an Italian transport of wounded? But I learned that at the border all soldiers were examined by the police. What if they asked him questions he could not answer in Italian? Then I thought, maybe he could wear a bandage around his neck and claim that he was shot in his throat and therefore could not speak. This had to be carefully arranged. I wondered how I could do it. I just did not know how to proceed. I was sure it could have successfully been planned if only I had some friends with whom I could discuss the matter.

One day I received a call at the Italian hospital from my mother's employer, Römer. He told me that my mother was ill with pneumonia and that he was taking her back to my father in the ghetto in Drohobycz. I ran quickly to see my mother. She looked terrible and was really glad to return. She just did not have the strength to continue the pretense. The superintendent of her building would always ask her many questions and looked at her in a highly suspicious way. Always being on guard really enervated her. I knew what she was going through because my situation was similar.

Nevertheless I did not want to return. I kissed my mother, not knowing if I would ever see her again.

Once in a while I would enter a church. I liked to sit there in the quiet peaceful atmosphere. I would look at the pictures of Christ and the Virgin Mary and think about my God. I could relax since no one would bother me there. It was wonderful to see paintings once again and to gaze upon beauty. Then I would think about Janowska. The people there, dead or living, were still an integral part of me. In my heart they would always remain alive.

### In The Hands of the Local Hoodlum

Two months later I volunteered to go to work in Germany. There was absolutely nothing else I could do. There was an increase in men who went through the town looking for Jews with Aryan papers. It was either a loosely or closely organized band, I never did know which. Their main source of income was dependent on finding Jews and blackmailing them for money not to denounce them to the Gestapo. Once I was on their list as a suspect it would be impossible to exist. No matter how much I paid to one of them, others would threaten. Twice I was confronted by a young man who knew me from the Polytechnik, possibly one of my colleagues, I did not remember. I paid him once, and then a second time I gave him everything I had in my purse that day, including some of my sister's jewelry which I carried with me. One man I paid off told me quite frankly that I should change my appearance. My green goat with the nutria collar, my hat to match and my golden curls were now recognizable by the gang. I felt like a trapped animal. I was still breathing but I was not sure from where the next blow would come.

Then one day when I gave a man some money to let me go, he took my purse and found my address. Now I knew that something bad would happen, but I did not know how to prevent it. Somehow, since the day I tried to kill myself in the general's apartment and survived, I felt rather stronger for the experience. I could not explain the change, but I was better able to endure all the many abuses now. All I could think of was that those men had my address and they knew where they could find me.

At about seven o'clock one evening in early May, I was sitting at the table in the kitchen mending my best dress, the printed silk one of my sister's. The only light in the kitchen was that supplied by a candle since this was the day when our side of the street was without electricity. I heard footsteps on the staircase. They came closer. I was listening, my heart pounding faster. I knew that people did not visit each other in the evenings. I was sure that someone was coming to get me. There was a knock at the door. I could not move. Stasia opened the door and two men entered. They were local people working for the Gestapo, they said, and wanted to see my papers. I let them have them. They then asked me for my name, the town in which I was born, and the name of the priest who baptized me. I had visualized a scene like this many times. I always feared that I would forget my new name, and telling them my old one. I lifted my head, looked at the two men and said, Krystyna Kozlowska. Of course I remembered everything. I was calm and poised and in control of myself. They told me to get dressed and said that they were taking me to the Gestapo. I dressed, put on my hat and coat, said goodbye to Stasia, who just whispered, "What could I do for you?" I really felt sorry for her, and walked out with my two interrogators into the pitch dark streets of Lwow. I took a deep breath of fresh air and said, "I am glad you are taking me to the Gestapo. I am happy that it is all over." The tall man said, "My God, you are so young, why do you want to die?" "I do not have any strength left," I said again. "Do you have any money or jewelry?" they asked. I gave them all that I had in my bag. This time it was everything I owned. It really was not much, the last small pieces of my sister's jewelry that my mother gave me and two hundred zlotys. They took it and said, "You have to disappear from Lwow. We will tell the Gestapo that you were not at home." I looked at them in disbelief. Then the taller man said, "You must not return to your apartment. You are coming with us." Then, surprisingly, he added, "I really like you—some day after the war I would like to marry you even though you are a Jew." I felt like laughing and crying at the same time. I wondered if I would have killed him if I had a gun. I never did find the answer. From the homes we were passing, through the blinded windows I could hear the voices of people talking, laughing, arguing, and singing and music. The people here seemed to be living a normal life. Only I was dying inside. Don't let them assault me, I prayed, but I knew that not all prayers were answered. Thank God I had loved before, deeply and beautifully, I thought. No matter what they do to me, it will not really matter, I kept repeating to myself.

The shorter man was married and the father of two. He was a chimney sweep before the war and now he was a big man working for the police, an important man, he thought. Another Jewish woman was in his apartment, caught in a different escapade and kept there instead of in prison because she was a dressmaker. His wife planned to keep her for the duration of the war. She wanted completely new wardrobes tailored for herself, her children and her best friends. What luck to be a seamstress, I thought. I felt that it would be best for me to leave Lwow and go to Warsaw to try to establish myself there. I knew that some of my father's relatives lived there with Aryan papers.

I contacted my parents by calling a highly trusted Polish man in Drohobycz who worked with my father. Not wishing to alarm them, I did not disclose the whole truth about my situation. I simply stated that I would like to leave Lwow for Warsaw and that I needed the address of our relatives there, and about 1,000 zlotys to be sent to the address of the short man. I always wondered what my parents thought really happened to me then, but I never asked. The next morning a young Pole whom my parents previously sent on similar chores brought me 1500 zlotys and the address of a Polish woman who might be helpful in arranging a meeting with my relatives.

I decided to leave for Warsaw a day later, but first I had to pick up my clothes. The short man accompanied me to my apartment. Stasia was there, along with some of the neighbors who looked at me in terror. Back at the chimney sweep's apartment, I gave the wife almost all of my clothes and kept only the most essential things that I was able to fit into a small suitcase. My dresses were immediately spread all over the floor to help me decide how the Jewish dressmaker should remake them. In their excitement the wife decided that perhaps her husband should bring me to Warsaw in order to make the journey safer for me. The money I had was sufficient for two fares.

I realized then, that these people were really not murderers, though I felt that they could easily kill if the situation became too dangerous. At this stage they were not interested in seeing me dead. Sometimes it seemed they even liked me and wished me well. But this was their new means of sustenance. Catching Jews and getting all that they could from them was the most lucrative source of income they ever had. They very probably wished that the war would continue for a long time. They even appraised my looks as an Aryan and agreed that I looked like one except for my eyes. They were "scared" eyes, Jewish eyes. These people were the experts. They felt I should relax and smile more while in the company of others.

I never knew "hoodlums" of this type before. Who were they, these people without any scruples? Not for a second could they understand what I was going through. Did they ever think about it? Were they even capable of thinking? I was totally bewildered by this time. When I was previously approached by some of these "denunciators" I never really knew who they were or how they operated. Now, after living in their presence, I was still in the dark and even more confused than ever. Yet I was able to discuss my plans completely and freely with them. Time was not of the essence for them. When they were not in "action" they would sit around and talk, eat and drink. But I was becoming quite nervous. At times I felt that I was going insane because of these people.

Besides the possibility of going to Warsaw, I was also considering another option, that of joining the partisans in the woods. I wanted very much to do it, and asked my "captors" how I could contact this group. It was generally known that they were concentrated around Kielce, directly on the road to Warsaw. That evening they asked a friend of theirs over, one who had some contacts among the partisans. They, of course, did not tell him that I was Jewish. The friend said that the only way I could arrange to meet them would be to jump off the train while passing the woods near Kielce, and then walk right into their camp. He also mentioned that the train would always slow down near the forest as there usually was some shooting in the area. During further conversation he told us stories about life among the partisans and some Jewish girls who, as he put it, served as "mattresses" for the men. I felt so hopelessly weak again. That was the end of my plan to join the partisans.

We arrived in Warsaw late in the afternoon and went straight to some friends of the short man. He introduced me as his wife's sister who came here with him to buy some goods that were not available in Lwow. That sounded like a usual activity in which the so-called "combinators" indulged during the war.

It was May 7. Warsaw was in an awful state, friends told us. Water and electricity were cut off because there was fighting going on in the ghetto. One of the women added, "Jewish mothers were throwing their babies over the wall so they wouldn't burn alive." She said this in a cold matter of fact fashion with no compassion or horror in her voice, in just a flat detached and indifferent statement. This was how I learned about the uprising in the ghetto.

The next morning I went to call on the woman whose address I received from home. She was originally from our town. Our parents were acquainted. I knew that she had helped some of my father's more distant relatives to settle in Warsaw as Aryans. The luxury of her one room studio apartment amazed me. I forgot what it meant to have silk comforters and beautiful draperies. My God, it was all so long ago. She was curling her hair when I came. Her somewhat mature male friend was watching her in the mirror. She did not stop working on her hair but was very polite and informed me in a forthright manner that she could obtain a Kennkarte for me and a ration book for any where between 8,000 to 10,000 zlotys.

That, however, was out of the question for me. I made my decision right there standing in front of the two of them. I knew I could get the money from my parents, but I would never ask. I wanted them to use their funds to save themselves or for members of our family who were older or younger than me. I did not feel my parents were my responsibility in this regard. They were still young, extremely able, and I knew that I could not contribute anything toward their safety and well being. On the contrary, I felt that because I was able to take care of myself I was alleviating this problem for them. I had helped them in any way I possibly could. but I certainly did not want their money.

When I arrived in Lwow I got my Kennkarte and ration book by myself, in a legitimate way by applying for it as any normal Aryan would. I was so terribly afraid of going through all those legal channels, but I managed. This was the most difficult way to establish oneself as an Aryan and hardly anyone attempted it the prescribed official way. Usually Poles were paid to obtain it for them. I did it once. Now I wanted to repeat it in Warsaw. But I needed a place to stay and some knowledge of the usual procedures required in Warsaw. There were problems in which the young woman was definitely not interested. She had so little time, as she confessed, curling her hair during the entire time she spoke with me. She and her companion were going to a party and I was really taking up too much of her time already. She felt that possibly her sister and brother who lived apart might direct me to the uncle of my father. He now lived with Aryan papers in Warsaw. She then gave me the address of her sister who I knew was married to a physician.

When I got to the sister's house, there were many people present, mostly family, since it was the birthday of her young son. The grandmother, the doctor's mother, arrived at the same time that I did. Through an open door I could hear the congratulations and see the kissing, the smiling happy faces, and a maid in a dark uniform wearing a white apron. Yes, the brother of the two sisters was also there. A bon vivant before the war, he looked the same as I remembered him, handsome and wearing a small moustache. He seemed a bit shocked when I told him who I was, but he behaved in a civilized manner. He left me standing at the door as he kissed the grandmother's hand in the usual European tradition. Then he turned to me and with an apologetic smile commented that I could see for myself how busy they were with the birthday party for the little boy. I smiled wanly, and asked for some addresses of my family which he claimed not to have. Usually my father's uncle would contact him, he said, but only when the need for additional papers arose. He smiled again and pointed out how busy he was because everyone was waiting for him to partake of the birthday cake. I returned his smile and left.

This scene of a normal family life at a time when our lives were being shattered, when the last of the survivors in the ghetto were facing death, left me drained. I thought about Oleś who was about the same age as the birthday boy, and about my grandparents, the ones who were killed and those still alive, probably somewhere in hiding. I felt very low. Again there were some weighty questions in my mind—was life really worth fighting for? Who were we anyhow, and why did so very few people identify with us? I went back to where I left my companion. He had waited there impatiently. With great excitement he pointed out to me that some of the people in the streets looked semitic. I could see that he wished I would disappear so that he could find an easy "kill." What madness. I was just too tired to talk. He decided to take the first train back to Lwow. On the way to the station I looked at Warsaw, at the children playing in the streets, the men and women walking around on this beautiful sunny day, a fine May day, and in the distance the ghetto. "Jewish mothers are throwing their children over the wall to prevent them from being burned alive." I heard it over and over again. If only somebody would end it for me—I had little energy left to try it myself once again. What was I supposed to do?

While in the train, I thought of a new possibility. I decided to leave Poland and go to Germany as a so-called "forced laborer." There were many advertisements in the papers for workers. Sometimes the Germans would send the population of entire villages. That would be my intention now, just to get out of Poland. I never heard about any of my Jewish friends going to Germany or even thinking about it. I personally never knew a Pole or a Ukrainian who went, but somehow the idea came to my mind, possibly out of sheer desperation. I told my companion about my new resolve. He did not object. He had learned everything he could from me. He knew that I had some money left from the original amount I received from my parents, but he was no longer interested in obtaining it. He had new plans. Those Jewish looking people in Warsaw—"Were they really Jewish?" he wondered once in the train. He told me that his colleagues once caught a German woman who had black hair and a likely semitic profile who they mistook for a Jew. He sighed and added, "Things are not always so easy." As with me? I wanted to ask. But now, regarding my future, he was just interested in my disappearance from Lwow so that in the event that I was caught by the Gestapo, I would not turn him in as a Jew hunter who did it to fill his pockets with money, instead of for the Gestapo.

During our leisurely discussion on the train, another alternative was mentioned by the short man, one which he and his friends provided for a girl they recognized as being Jewish. They, his friends and he, rented a room and helped the girl to establish herself as a prostitute, he said. They all patronized her and helped her as much as they could, he assured me. He saw nothing wrong with it. He added, "another way to survive the war." She was a very young high school girl, with no family. She managed to run away from the vicinity of Sambor the day her parents were deported. She had no one left, no one to whom she could turn.

At the station in Lwow I said goodbye to my companion. I could not possibly face him or his family for another minute. I quickly bought a paper. Yes, the advertisement for work in Germany was still there—"young intelligent Polish girls wanted for work in

Bavaria." I was suddenly energized. I went directly to the Arbeits-amt [Employment Office] with my suitcase and said that I was applying for the job. It was so easy: I showed my Kennkarte and my passport. I was all set. They really needed and wanted those girls to work in Germany! All the necessary papers were filled out while I waited. The only problem was that the next transport was not scheduled to leave for another ten days. Where was I supposed to stay until then? Suddenly I had an idea. I would hide in the Italian hospital where I previously worked. I could probably ask the girls who were there for help. I then went directly from the Arbeitsamt to the hospital. I passed the guards who knew me, and found the Russian girls. I briefly told them my story and they were pleased to accomodate me there.

I confided to the Russian girls, with a pounding heart, that I was Jewish and that I was escaping to Germany because I could no longer find a hiding place in Poland. They said quietly that they knew it all along having been told by the Ukrainian girl who switched jobs with me. She was the one who took my shoes and of whom I was always afraid. Here I was pre-tending, trying so hard to hide my true identity, and yet so many total strangers knew who I was. Fortunately not one of them denounced me, not even the Ukrainian girl or her policeman friend. As usual, my intuition deceived me. I could never sense who was a friend or who an enemy, but I know that other people must have made even worse judgmental mistakes. One after another, my closest girl friends were being caught by the Ukrainian police or were being betrayed and seized by the Gestapo. They were often first raped by the local police, by as many as forty men, and then they were turned over to the Germans.

I stayed in one room then with Sonia, Svetlana, and Tania. I knew them quite well since I had previously worked with them for some time, but we were never too close. Now during these eight days I would learn a great deal more about them. Sonia, a teacher of the history of Marxism, was tall, slim, dark-haired, and needed a man every night. Svetlana was a student of coal mining engineering. She was blonde, beautiful, and she was preserving her virginity for a handsome prince. She was proud of her hard, pear-shaped breasts, afraid that any sexual relationship would make them less firm. Tania, a medical student from Moscow, was the least attractive of the three but very humane and easier to understand. Just as I had previously done, the girls, myself and some of the nuns peeled potatoes for about ten hours a day interspersed with the chanting of prayers.

The war provided the first encounter with Christianity for the Russian girls. In their home town after the German occupation, they were paid to go to church. They fell in love with some Italians who fought with the Germans. As the Axis army retreated after Stalingrad and being afraid of Soviet reprisals for possible collaboration with the enemy, the girls followed the Italian troops to Lwow. They were promised by their lovers and admirers another trip to Italy, marriage, and a good life. While listening to prayers to Christ or the Virgin Mary both the sisters Sonia and Svetlana remarked, amusedly, "What beautiful children's fables." "Fables," screamed the horrified nuns. "Of course, these are only stories for the young. You cannot convince us that you adults take them seriously," answered the astonished Russian girls.

I tried to convince Sonia that as long as she enjoyed men's company so much, it could be more interesting for her to have a relationship with a lieutenant. They were generally more refined and intelligent men than the cooks and privates with whom she slept. Education and social standing meant nothing, the Marxist teacher assured me; only the virility of the men mattered and that was not dependant on one's education. She made her point. Experience was important, I admitted. I became very fond of those girls. Why didn't I expend more effort to get to know any of those who came to Lwow in 1939, I thought. I did not really give them a chance. Now they were my saviors.

### On the Way to Germany

The day of my departure for Germany arrived. In the morning of May 22 I was told to report to the Janowska Concentration Camp where the preparatory examinations were to take place. It was the same Janowska, but it certainly had changed. Now it was a town unto itself. The side building to which I came was not even on the grounds I had known previously, but it probably was not too far from where all the daily killings took place. I wondered if someone would recognize me. Perhaps some policemen that I once knew.

As I entered the building all the faces of the Ukrainian and German SS looked unfamiliar to me and I felt relieved. First, our vaginas were examined, for possible syphilis infection I assumed. And here the nightmare began. The medical examinations took place in open rooms in the presence of Ukrainian policemen in uniforms and some civilians who were talking, laughing, and at times not even paying attention to the girls being tested before their very eyes. It must have become a rather routine matter for them. Then the main event started. All the women bound for the transport were ordered to undress and march in a circle in front of the doctors with a minimum of privacy from the now more interested local policemen and civilians. I could not believe it. After all, we were not in prison. The civilians, mostly local trash, showed off as their way of celebrating the war. What was the conflict doing to those people? We dressed, and as we were all evidently approved, we were directed to a large hall with wooden benches, where the men who were also leaving joined us. We were told to wait to find out when our trains would depart.

Here I met the girls who were supposed to accompany me in a group—the "intelligent Polish girls wanted for work in Bavaria." There were two Marys, a short and a tall one, and a Victoria. The short Mary with braids around her head was a mere child who did not look to be more than fifteen years of age. The tall Mary, a woman of perhaps thirty with short black hair and a long narrow face, definitely appeared quite sure of herself in a black leather jacket. She really frightened me. Wherever I moved her eyes followed me, always with a questioning and searching look. She was the one who suggested that we sing Christmas carols, almost as if she knew that I had neither a singing voice, or that I could not participate in the caroling, or that I also believed singing Christmas songs in May was ridiculous. It seemed that the entire group of people were going to different parts of Germany, some two hundred perhaps, were just waiting for the chance; and they all joined in enthusiastically.

I was getting a painful migraine headache and my throat hurt. I really felt sick. Suddenly a few civilians approached me and asked, "What's your name?" I answered, "Krystyna Kozlowska," and they continued to ask all the usual questions employed by the denunciators: From which Kozlowskas are you descended, where is your family from, and so on and so on. I answered, "From some not very

important ones." One ugly looking short man was particularly
insistent. I could sense that he did not believe a word I was saying.
Finally another Ukrainian who stood aside before, came forward
and spoke for me. He was a tall young man with kind blue eyes.
He looked at me carefully as I whispered, "I have a terrible headache, could you give me an aspirin?" The ugly one answered,
"Girl, I do not believe that an aspirin will solve your problems." At
that, the young man said in a very quiet but strong voice, "Leave
her alone." From their agitated conversation I learned that a few
days earlier a young girl from Stanislawow was also rudely interrogated by these men. Since she was apparently Jewish, she started to
run and was shot by a policeman right in the same room in which
we were. The tall man was saying, "Do you want all that blood
here again?" and then added, "Leave her alone." To my surprise
the interrogator retreated.

The nice man sat near me on the bench and said, "I will take
care of you until the trains for Germany leave." "When will that
be?" I asked. "Not until tomorrow noon." Dear God, I thought, I
had a whole night to wait with all those men present! It seemed
like a nightmare with all of them staring at me, some with approval
and some not; it really didn't matter by then. My headache was
unbearable, and the dark haired girl was still singing her carols. I
just did not believe that I could survive even the few hours before
nighttime. And what will happen to me this night? How many will
assault me? What was this nice man expecting in return?

Suddenly everybody jumped up. The news spread in second—
the trains would be moving shortly. We were to hurry to the
railroad station just a few blocks away without delay. I truly
thought that this was the greatest miracle in the world. Trains were
usually late, but never a day early. They must have selected a
different train for our transport. I believed that it was done just for
me. "Dear God, thank you," I repeated over and over. The nice
Ukrainian said he would bring me to the station so that no harm
would come to me. All at once my gratefulness to him was overwhelming, especially now that I was leaving and the nightmare was
coming to an end. I quickly offered him a small additional passport
photo I carried in my bag. On the other side I wrote, "I will be
grateful to you always, K.K." We arrived at the station, the man
helped me to enter the wagon, and said, "Now you are safe, good
luck," and left. There followed the conductor's whistle. Just at this

moment the other man, my oppressor, jumped up to the window and shouted, "Give me your suitcase or I will pull you off the train." I gave him my suitcase through the window while the train was beginning to roll. He had overlooked my handbag in which I had a few pictures and some money.

I looked through the window at the disappearing Lwow station, not believing that I had really succeeded. The train was really moving. I would not have to spend the night among these men. "Thank you, God," was all I could think of at this moment. I always thanked Him for the good things, and I continually prayed in despair, but never under normal circumstances from childhood to the present. Just then I heard a voice behind me saying, "Don't move, just listen. I am so glad you managed. I know you are Jewish. I am Jewish too. We have to leave the train before some of the others get suspicious." It was the tall dark haired woman talking, the one I feared so much. Again, my early perceptions were wrong. In the next few minutes she told me her whole life story—very rich parents, owners of a factory, a lawyer husband killed by the Germans. She found another man with whom she fell in love and was going to try to bring him to Germany as soon as she got there. She was also going to Bavaria, to Mittenwald, as a "young intelligent Polish girl . . ."

My whole life changed. Even my headaches disappeared. I had a friend with whom I could talk, and she was accompanying me to Germany. I was no longer alone. If only I could have told my parents, I thought. My new friend told me that she noticed a man who came to our group recently and was not subjected to all the preliminary checks. A young Pole was examined instead; just before we boarded the train he disappeared, and the other one took his place. How many more, we wondered, escaped from Poland in this way? If only my parents would dare, I thought. But the risk was enormous, and the precision needed to plan the whole operation was a difficult but necessary factor. Good will and money were also necessary. Nerves had to be sure and steady.

"Big" Mary, as we called her, convinced "little" Mary and Victoria that we should separate from the large "slave" transport and move on our own to Bavaria, especially since we had our tickets. The other girls agreed so readily that the two of us began to think that perhaps they too were Jewish. However, we could not risk asking them in the event they were not. We quietly left our train when it stopped in Krakow and boarded a German military transport which was going in the same westward direction. The German military men, mostly high ranking officers, did not object to our presence. The conductor who checked our tickets for Bavaria when the train was already in motion, told us to change in Czechoslovakia. When we arrived at Pilzen he left with us and showed us where to board a train for Vienna and then Bavaria. If he only knew to whom he was so polite!

I was once again going to Vienna, my Vienna, only it was not really mine any longer. Many thoughts passed through my mind, my happy childhood, my grandparents' apartment on Hermangasse, the big doll store, and the Kunsthistorische and Naturhistorische Museum with all its beautiful stones and pictures. I was finally going there after all the nightmares I had endured.

The station in Vienna was crowded with soldiers. It was evening when we arrived. We sat at a table, ordered some coffee and were offered some sugar by an old soldier. He then he gave each of us a piece of bread for which we were normally required to have coupons. There was no food at the station, but nothing really mattered. We spent the night sleeping on the benches. The next day I gave the girls a tour of Vienna. We walked and walked for hours. We passed near the Opera and Burg theater and looked at the sparse window displays at Gerngross and Herzmansky showing just a few notebooks and pencils. We saw signs throughout the city reading "Juden verboten" [Jews forbidden]. I had seen them before, but it still shocked me. It was definitely not my Vienna anymore. What in this big wide world was mine?

In the evening we left for Bavaria. Our next night was spent in Weilheim in a large camp for foreign workers. We were informed by the camp physician that if we wanted to have any kind of relationship it could only be with him as all the Frenchmen in camp suffered from venereal diseases. He was an Italian. Needless to say, we thanked him sincerely for his offer. We parted with Victoria and did not see her again. She made no attempt to contact us. I was really interested in knowing who she really was, since I was quite sure that she was not the prim lady she pretended to be. But then, all my intuitions invariably proved to be wrong. "Big" Mary left the train the next day in Mittenwald and "little" Mary parted tearfully in Garmisch-Partenkirchen and begged me to contact her as soon as possible. I hardly had any doubts about her identity. As young and as well bred as she was, she was not likely to have ever volunteered to go to work in Germany, if she knew of another way out. If only she were not so stubborn or so frightened to speak out, the next two long years of her life might not have been so difficult.

My final destination was Oberammergau, where I arrived in the evening. The countryside was beautiful. The peaks of the mountains were covered with snow. Below were forests and a river. Everywhere were the wood-constructed Bavarian homes and men and women in their native Tyrolean-like costumes. I was met at the station by Herr König, the owner of the Bahnhof Gaststätte, for whom I was supposed to be the "Zwang Arbeiterin" "slave worker." The last bus for Oberammergau had already left, and my employer informed me that we had to walk up the mountain. I wore high heeled shoes which originally were my sister's. My own everyday shoes were in my suitcase somewhere in Lwow. I wore my sister's gray woolen suit made in 1936 from English material, which was still beautiful; it was the only suit I brought with me. Mr. König asked me where my suitcase was and I told him that I had lost it. Those were the only words we exchanged during our two and a half hour walk. He was a sour looking little man in his leather pants, furious that I had arrived so late and that we had to do all this walking. After some time, I took off my shoes and proceeded barefoot. It was more comfortable than wearing my high heels.

It was about midnight when we reached Oberammergau. The whole Bahnhoff Gaststätte, the small hotel with the restaurant at the train station which was now to be my new home and place of employment, was completely dark. In the dimly lit kitchen the old grandfather was waiting for us, with two black cats sitting near the stove. I was very tired, bewildered, and I suddenly felt very lonely and lost. I thought, What was I doing here? All my earlier excitement vanished. Here I was in a German hotel-restaurant with unpleasant Germans who hardly spoke with me, and so far away from the ones I loved. I went upstairs to the room I was supposed to share with another Polish worker, Stacha, a peasant girl, who was very pretty. She rose from the bed when I entered and in a peasant dialect lamented, "Oh Jesus, how awful it is here, so much work, so much work." Then she informed me that the next day,

Sunday, we had to rise at five in the morning to scrub all the floors. Sunday was a busy day in the restaurant, and everything had to be particularly clean for the arriving guests. This was the routine. I could hardly reach the bed. Before I fell asleep my last thoughts were of Drohobycz and Boryslaw. They seemed so far away, exactly 1500 kilometers from Lwow, as my ticket indicated.

# 4

· · · · ·

# Oberammergau

The small village of Oberammergau was inhabited by four kinds of people. The main group, the villagers, were all involved, in one way or another, with the Passion plays. Some were actors, elderly bearded men who were exempted from the army and who would just ready themselves for the next play after the war, of course. These were the village's personalities. Mrs. König would always point them out to me with great excitement, "Look, look! That is ... Joseph or Judas." Whenever a few of the local people gathered they would, after all the complaints about food shortages were over, talk constantly about the plays. They missed the crowds that previously came to see their famous performances, mostly the English tourists.

We were among the second group of inhabitants of the village, — "the Auslanders" or "foreigners." In a way it seemed that they were waiting for every one of us, as if we were part of their precious lives before the war. Oberammergau must have been one of the few places where Germans loved to hear foreign languages spoken loudly in their streets. Little old ladies from tobacco or little gift shops always sighed when they heard or saw us. "Oh the Auslanders are here again." They would treat us as welcome guests in their stores, not as "forced laborers." We could stay in their shops for as long as we wanted touching and looking at the little carved wooden animals made by local craftsmen. Time and again we would hear the same story about how the English used to buy them. There was no market for them now, but they were content to have us admire them.

The Auslanders were brought from all over German-occupied Europe, in most cases as forced laborers. At times there were also voluntary Polish villagers among my co-workers who thought they would find a better life here than the one they led at home. The Germans would often deport the inhabitants of entire villages. This happened in the little town in which the Russian girls came to work at the hotel. Most of the French employees were prisoners-of-war who lived in the POW camps, but who, during the day, performed many duties in Oberammergau, among them collecting garbage. Another group of French laborers were those who, for one reason or another, wanted to leave France, or that is what I thought, though I was never sure. Much later, after the Badoglio uprising of 1943, Italians by the hundreds were seized. They enlivened the inhabitants with their constant singing. After the Warsaw uprising in 1944 dozens of Poles were also sent to Oberammergau. There were some Czechs too, who had come here earlier.

The foreigners in Oberammergau could hardly communicate with each other; and the German they had learned as time passed was not sufficient to determine differences in intelligence, social standing or breeding. It was really amusing to observe the sophisticated Frenchman talking with a young Russian girl who had never left her native town. This happened to Stacha, the girl who worked with me. She was very pretty, her face was beautifully shaped, her skin translucent, her eyes, greenish-blue and her long hair a chestnut brown. She could barely read or write, and she admitted it freely—"something was wrong with her head." The village teacher sent her home when she was in the second grade, and that was the end of her education. One of the French workers became quite interested in her and asked me to find out from Stacha if she could play the piano well. I bit my lip and said, "I think not so very well." He was a college student from a French aristocratic family in Lyon. If he could only hear the words from Stacha's mouth when things were not going well in our kitchen. This, I learned, was a main characteristic of those peasant girls. When all went well, they were pleasant and likeable enough; but, God forbid, when matters got out of control—then the whole lack of proper upbringing would become blatantly evident. I found it fascinating to observe.

Even more pronounced and interesting were the national differences among the prisoners or "forced" laborers from each particular country which became quite noticeable in their daily behavior. For example, food was scarce for all the workers. When Italians came to the back door of the restaurant, they would beg, "Beautiful Senorita, could you give us something to eat?" The Czechs and the Poles would never ask, they were too proud. The Russians would come wearing their warm hats, even in the summer, and ask if they could do some chores for a meal. The Frenchmen knew how and did it best. They would have a lady friend in every restaurant and in many private German homes while the husbands were away. At times, I really thought that some of them were there especially to keep the beds warm until the heroic husbands returned. Each nationality reflected their own distinct customs.

The third group was a transient one. They were the "Prussians," (the "Berliners") and other Germans, mostly women and children sent here from other parts of Germany where the bombing was the heaviest. Some of them were wives or, in a few cases, as we found out, sweethearts of some high officials. For a few months at a time, they would stay in our hotel at the station, and then we would learn all the details. Their houses were bombed, and their husbands were usually in the Gestapo in Warsaw, Krakow or elsewhere. I would just look at them without saying a word—I could imagine what their men were doing. The women were frustrated, spoiled creatures, producing children for their husbands or sweethearts and mostly for their Führer. They were really longing for their men or any men, as we soon learned. They would give their children aspirins at night so they would sleep soundly; then the women would leave to meet some German soldiers on furlough or even more happily French workers in town. They very seldom chose mates of any other nationality.

The owner of our Gaststätte was a prude, as all Oberammergauers were "saint-people" because of their passion plays, of course. We would all laugh. He noticed what was taking place, and one early morning at about four o'clock we heard shouting. There was Mr. König standing with a broom in his hand at the entrance door to the hotel threatening to beat the returning "Prussian" women if they dared to leave at night again. From then on, all the doors were locked at ten o'clock in the evening. The women begged us, at times, to leave one small window open in a side bathroom through which they could crawl. We did it gladly as the morality of the German ladies was definitely not our concern.

Then there were the Messerschmitt workers who came to work every day by bus and train to the airplane factories camouflaged in the mountains of Oberammergau. They arrived by the thousands. They ate in our restaurant and in all the other dining places in the town where other foreign workers were employed. We would serve between one hundred to two hundred meals in the evening before they all departed for the night. The rush hours were wild because all train and bus schedules had to be met.

The morality of the Oberammergauers bordered on puritanism, and they loved to exhibit it freely. They tried to influence others to accept their mode of living, but in the end they proved to be not so pure, as we cursorily observed, or heard about from the local gossips. But these were their own affairs and not to be revealed to outsiders. For those they devised strict rules. They decided that the women workers and men who worked at the Messerschmitt factory should live in separate villages. At night, the women were driven by bus to Ethal and the men to Oberau, or to different towns, but always totally segregated.

My adjustment to the new surroundings was painfully slow. About a year after my arrival Stacha told me, "You know, when you first came I thought that you were not altogether sane." "Touched," she would add. "You jumped when someone addressed you. You became apprehensive when you heard footsteps on the stairs." How right she was. I'm still frightened when I hear those steps. One of the girls watched me one day while I was wringing out a large rag. I sopped up the water from the wooden floor after scrubbing it with a brush with soap and rinsing. She looked and said sarcastically, "you wring out the rag like a Jew . . ." If you only knew, I thought.

The work was difficult and very taxing at the start. I would wash the dishes in the basement. They came down on an elevator operated manually. They kept coming almost endlessly, and after the dishes came the large pots. I was often there until midnight when I finally went to bed and fell asleep. I would dream about huge amounts of dishes falling all over me.

Later, three other girls were assigned to help us. Zocha was Polish, about seventeen. Two Russian sisters were thirteen and fifteen years respectively. The older one was a capable seamstress, as were all the Russian girls I met previously. They were extremely pleasant, and as they were so young we would take care of them. We would allow them to sleep longer in the morning because we felt they needed it—they were still growing.

After a few months one of the waitresses became ill. My employer asked me to serve food in the restaurant. The "Auslanders" ate in one large room. With my knowledge of foreign languages I was able to communicate with them in a much better way than were the German girls. I became a waitress only when food was served, but in the morning from five until late at night, I still had all the other chores to finish. Cooking for 200 people was quite an experience—"Eintopfgericht" or "Himmel und Erde" (potatoes and applesauce), pigs in a blanket, meatloaf, stew, and huge quantities of each.

Twice the Königs had a pig killed by a friendly butcher right in the celler to keep from sharing it with the authorities. We all worked through that whole night. By early morning all the sausages were done. I loved to see the Germans defying the rules.

When I received my first letter from my parents I trembled when I opened it. For two months I had not heard anything about them. As König handed it to me he commented, "Finish washing the clothes first . . . and then you will have time to read." I must have looked at him with such an expression of hatred and disgust that he retreated without a word and I ran upstairs to my room to read. I was quite nervous when I opened their letter and could hardly read through my tears. My wonderful parents wrote as if they were peasants. Since mostly Polish peasant girls went to work in Germany, they were afraid that they might endanger my stay there in the event that the letter was opened. They never realized that I did not even pretend to be a peasant. I explained to my parents in my next letter so that they would not worry about writing more freely. My father informed me that the cows were doing fine, and then wrote about every peasant "girl-friend" of mine who was with him while he wrote the letter, giving them the names of my aunts and cousins to reassure me that they were still all right. Then my dearest mother added her well-written portion; she was always a gifted writer. She described how my uncle brought her a piece of linen which he wove himself and how she sewed a dress for me and that she was sending it immediately. She mentioned some other "home made" things she was sending as gifts from other members of my family, who missed me very much. I cried for an hour. There were were all thinking and worrying about me, sending me a dress when they themselves were in such a critical situation. My father again mentioned the name of the Pole to whom I was to write in order to reach them and to make it seem less suspicious, called him "my boy friend whom, he admonished me, to forget." I spent the whole night tearfully writing my letter to them and my heart was breaking. I longed for them so much. The next day my eyes were so red and swollen that I had to invent a tooth infection as the cause.

The most peaceful, rejuvenating experience during the time I spent in Oberammergau was a climb of the mountain Kofel. I always walked alone or with the König's dog as my companion. It would take me one hour to reach the top and from there, by holding on to a chain, I would climb up the rocky peak. The sky and clouds seemed so near. I felt so close to my parents, to all my family and friends, to my hometown, and again to Janowska. I would sometimes sit there for an hour just daydreaming and gazing at the sky. A metal box contained a book for tourists to sign. On one of my expeditions, I wrote the name of Ludka, Broyslaw, Poland. Kofel was my mountain, but the others felt it was dangerous for a girl to climb alone. König half-jokingly asked if I was meeting some dissident there.

I wished so much that I had known some of them. I once tried to mention rather casually to a French war prisoner that Germany was a good place to hide, but he never picked up on it. Politics was not a topic about which the prisoners were interested in talking. Then one day a French worker was arrested by the Gestapo. He was one of the bus drivers who brought the Messerschmitt workers to and from work. I knew him well, but he was the last one in whom I would confide, the last one I would suspect of illegal activities.

Thank God I was rather plain looking, pleasing enough to have around, but definitely not the Mata Hari type. I often believed this saved me. I was pleasant to be with but not to die or kill for. Also, I never looked like someone who might do something illegal, as for example, a Jew hiding in Oberammergau. Even at Janowska some of the Germans would look at me and say, "What a pity you are a Jew." They never went any further since there were enough exciting non-Jewish girls to choose from. In this respect I felt safe there. The Germans were not allowed to assault Jewish women as it could have resulted in a transfer to the Russian front for the perpetrators, or at least that is what I thought. Much later I learned that many Jewish girls were sent to bordellos to serve as prostitutes for the German soldiers. Thank God I never experienced that during the war. I did know the fate of many of my closest friends from Boryslaw and Lwow: nearly all of the most attractive, courageous ones, the intrigue types who drew attention to themselves, were dead by then. I was grateful for my plainness, or was remaining alive really that important while so many others died? We all fought for life so tenaciously just because the Germans decided we were not worthy to live. The importance of one's life during the war seemed unbelievably great to everyone I knew or observed. I once saw a mother in the ghetto frantically hiding hours after her five-year-old daughter was taken from her, just to survive even with a broken heart.

At times, "Big" Mary and I would meet on our days off and wander through the streets of Mittenwald or Oberammergau enchanted with the beauty of the countryside, but our hearts were in our home towns in Poland. We devised a game—who did this or that person remind us. We would take turns to tell our stories to each other about members of our family, friend or teacher of whom a particular German reminded us. We never tired of talking about the people at home. Sometimes we would also visit "little" Mary, but she never revealed her true identity. What a strong character that girl had.

"Big" Mary managed to send documents from her employers to a lawyer friend of hers in Krakow stating that he was needed for work in a hotel in Bavaria. The man, after miraculously substituting for some Poles during checking and examining procedures, made his way to Garmisch-Partenkirche. He was working as a porter at Zugspitze Hotel, a resting place for the highest ranking Gestapo members. It was situated on the top of a mountain which was always covered with snow. I went there twice with Mary to visit him. He prepared sun chairs for us on the terrace; and there, among the elite of the Gestapo, the three of us talked, not believing that this was really happening to us. More often, however, I went to Munich, the town I very much wanted to visit since long before

the war. Munich always seemed to me to be the cradle of civilization. I believed that there were old paintings to be discovered, and
valuable old books, and many great artists and writers. Whenever I
went to Munich on my free days I would run through the streets of
the city as if I were a child still playing in Vienna or Venice with
my family.

I continued to visit Munich even during the last month of the
war when the Allied bombs were dropping daily. I never believed
that an American or English bomb could hit me. One day while I
was having coffee in a "Liliput" restaurant the sirens started to
wail, I ran to a shelter near the station. It was amazing how orderly
the people entered the bunker, how quietly they sat while the
bombs exploded one after another. During this bombardment the
Liliput restaurant I was in a short time ago, was totally demolished.
I was elated to see the continuing destruction of Germany. My
heart sang with joy with every terrifying sound. I kept hoping
for more.

During one of my trips I sat in a train next to a German soldier.
He started a conversation asking where I was from. I answered,
from France, as Polish workers were not allowed to travel by train
in Germany without special permission. My companion assured
me that he heard how beautiful France was and then started
talking about his own trips abroad. "I was in Poland, Fraulein," he
said. "What aŋ awful and dirty country, and those Poles, just
pigs, just pigs." Somehow this statement coming from a German
infuriated me. From the way he looked at me I could see that he
did not really dislike me, and this buoyed me with courage. I
looked straight into his eyes and said, "I would just like you to
know that I am Polish and not French," and explained my reason
for lying. He became very apologetic. He assured me he was
only generalizing and there were many exceptions to the rule.
Then to emphasize his point he said, "Let us now talk about that
most awful people, the Jews. They should disappear from this
earth." He went on and on. My heart was sinking and I was
consumed with helpless anger. I yearned to say to him, look here, I
am really Jewish, not French, not Polish, but Jewish—but that
would mean my death. I asked him very quietly, "Why do you
think Jews are so awful?" He answered, "Oh, Fraulein, it was only
because of the Jews that Germany was so poor before Hitler. If it
were not for the Jews no German would every go hungry. If it were

not for them my father would not have been a lowly clerk but the owner of a store," and he continued in this vein. The propaganda teachings were effective! For the remainder of the trip I pretended to be asleep.

One day Mr. König accompanied me to Munich. He wanted me to buy foreign cigarettes for him on the black market where only "Auslanders" were allowed to enter and exchange or buy goods. I never knew that such a place existed. It was amazing to see what the foreign workers brought here. The most wonderful merchandise was offered by the French, perfumes, silk stockings, shoes, but the prices were astronomically high. I bought cigarettes for my boss, and for myself I decided on a black dress with a white lace collar. I did not know then that this would someday be my wedding dress.

On one of my other trips, not far from Munich, the train suddenly slowed down. I looked through the window and saw men repairing the railroad tracks. They all wore striped uniforms. Their heads were shaved, and they wore caps. I started to tremble. Who were they, I thought? I looked around and all the German travelers were also watching. The talking subsided. One could hear people breathing. Only later did I learn that they were most probably inmates from Dachau. I knew or heard little about Dachau while in Oberammergau and never realized that this camp was so close by.

On a sunny day in summer, again on my day off, I went to Murnau. I had heard that this was the place where Polish prisoners were being held. First, I wanted to visit them, but then I thought that perhaps someone would recognize me. I then rented a boat and started rowing to a small island located on the side of a beautiful lake. Suddenly I noticed a few men in striped suits and caps. I came closer, but still maintained a safe distance. I was afraid to come ashore on this place. The men noticed me, they looked in my direction and I looked back. Somehow I could not run from the spot. I was waiting and thinking about what I would do if I recognized a friend or a relative. I studied every face, but alas, they were all strangers.

A few weeks after I arrived in Oberammergau, the Königs asked me, when no one was in the kitchen, if there were concentration camps in Poland. I told them that the only one I had seen—I added that it was far away—was in Lwow, and that I had heard about one in Lublin. Everyone seemed to be sure that there were many more only I did not know where. They asked more questions but never related them directly to the subject of Jews. On one occasion they mentioned that the Mayor of Oberammergau was Jewish and added in a whisper, "We do not know what happened to him."

There was one other remark Mrs. König made about Jews, which alone could have justified my hatred for her, although in a way I was sorry because she was otherwise a rather likeable person. She owned two black cats that she adored, and they would scamper all over the kitchen. Sometimes, when she was busy with a great deal of cooking, she would put them outside, but with each opening of the door they would jump back in. She once commented, referring to one of the cats, "You are like a Jew—thrown out through one window you keep coming back through another." The cat did not live long but this was not my vendetta. It was my free day, and I was still upstairs in the morning. Zocha ran in screaming, "The cat, the cat." I came running down and there was the cat, dead in the big stove. It seemed that she liked the warmth of the stove, and would jump into it at night. This time Zocha did not remember to let her out of the oven when she started the fire. I felt sick to my stomach. It was Stacha who saved the day. She removed the cat with a shovel and buried her deep into the garbage. For days Mrs. König speculated on what might have happened to the cat. She finally decided that the Italian prisoners killed and cannibalized her. She disliked the Italians and added, "they were eating frogs for a long time, so why not cats?"

As the war progressed, I was to experience many nerve-wracking situations with the Königs. They asked me to listen to the Italian announcements on the radio at the time of the collapse of Mussolini and to translate these for them into German. The same request was made for D-Day. Later, when we were all together in the kitchen we heard the report that there was an unsuccessful attempt on Hitler's life. We were all excited in various ways, always masking our true feelings carefully, and yet we were not particularly hostile towards each other. They knew how I felt and vice versa. Interestingly enough there were no tears in their eyes when Hitler was almost killed, not even a tiny hint of a let-down when it became known that the attempt did not succeed. After D-Day, when I was bursting with joy and excitement, they seemed terribly nervous, but very controlled. They became extremely polite towards me and the other girls.

At times the townsmen were called to help the police when there was an escape from the prisoner of war camps. They would all flee toward the Swiss border. Once König spent an entire night in the woods looking for two Russian officers, but they were never found. The civilian population was also ordered to look for American or English fliers who were shot down. We, the foreigners, looked for them also, dreaming and hoping to find them, to protect them in hiding, but it never happened in Oberammergau. In Munich after a heavy bombing, a plane was shot down. A black flyer was captured by the Germans. The population stoned him. A few days later the police caught an American flyer who parachuted in the vicinity of Oberammergau. They brought him to our restaurant for a few minutes while waiting for the train. He never raised his eyes but just kept staring at the floor. With the exception of a slight limp, he appeared healthy. How I wished some of we "Auslanders" could have found him. I watched when he was taken to the train bound for Munich, and I silently wished him well from the depths of my heart.

We dreamed of so many things. In the earlier period when I was still receiving letters from my parents, my father encouraged me to escape to Switzerland through the city of Constance. He wished so earnestly for me to get out of Germany. He wrote this in a very contrived manner so that no one would be able to understand its message but me. I started to inquire about the border, never from local people but from the transient soldiers. I learned that this would be an extremely dangerous attempt because even the Swiss were not too eager to accept refugees, particularly since the borders were well patrolled by the Germans.

For many months I did not hear from my parents. The last card I received was written on May 27, 1944, and it was almost impossible for me to decipher.* It stated that they were at the home of a friend of Stasia's, which meant in a house of a Polish woman, something I was unable to guess at the time. It went on to say that some other members of our family had managed to find hiding places for themselves while all the others were brought together near Elzunia's pre-war home, which indicated that they were in Auschwitz. Thank Gos I could not figure that out either. That was the last time I heard from them. I was completely cut off from

---

*See Appendix p. 141.

Poland. I resisted the thought that they might have perished. However, this terrible fear was always with me. Where were Zosia, Walterek, little Oles, Elzunia and all the others? How could my world exist without them and all my dearest friends?

One day I asked a soldier on furlough about what was going on in Poland, and then, summoning all my courage I asked rather casually: "What is happening to the Jews there?" He looked at me and said in a loud off-hand manner, "Oh the Jews, they must have all been slain by this time. I believe that not one of them remains alive." He said it as if he had never given some thought as to just what his statement implied—murder many fold. Everyone in the kitchen could hear him, but no one commented, not the Königs or the few strangers who were there. I had to suppress my screams. "My God! You are so young, so human in every other respect. How can you make such a statement so thoughtlessly?" I was afraid to look at the Königs lest I betray my feelings so apparent in my eyes, or to speak up, not sure if I could control my voice. After that, when I met "big" Mary we could no longer play our games. We couldn't help wondering, "Are we the only Jews left?" How can we face life alone? That seemed too cruel, too unbelievably inhumane, a thought we quickly shunted aside. "Dear God," I prayed, "you must save all my dear ones."

## The End is Coming

As unbelievable as it seemed, the war was coming to an end. The roaring planes flew over us day and night, sometimes quite low. We would wave excitedly, repeating words they could obviously not hear but we hoped that they could somehow sense: "We are here, we are praying for you. Please succeed for us, and most of all for all of our dear ones in Poland." The planes just kept flying.

By the late winter of 1944, railroad communications, as even we were aware, had been completely disrupted. Once a train loaded with butter intended for another town in Germany was stalled at our station for days. Finally, the villagers were allowed to unload it. More and more Germans from Berlin and northeastern Germany fled to Bavaria. In mid-April of 1945, SS men with their families passed through Oberammergau looking for ways to get out of Germany. They were all fleeing from the Russians. One day a large sack fell out of a car driven by a high ranking Gestapo man and many pounds of coffee spilled all over the road. That was really an event to make the Bavarians scream with rage—bean coffee in bags when all they ever had was an "ersatz" product for years! News reached Oberammergau that in Prussia even eighty year old women were being raped by the Russians. "How happy those Prussian women must be," callously remarked Mrs. König. Then she would add, "Oh you do not know them; they are all like that." She was trying to put some distance between herself and the Berliners, at least that was the impression she wanted to convey to us.

In their tremendous excitement some of the foreign workers decided to leave their jobs and move closer to the front lines to be among the first to greet the Allied forces. All at once every day of our stay with the Germans seemed impossible to endure, and no one wanted to work the sixteen or eighteen hour long days. I was so deeply interested in observing the behavior of the Germans in these last days that I really did not mind staying on. One morning, only days before the end of the war, two high ranking elderly German colonels entered our restaurant and asked for something to eat. One of them said, "There is no place for us to ruin to, Fraulein, we are surrounded on all sides." Their lives ere coming apart. I felt just the smallest bit of remorse, but I was really elated to hear those words. Once again I believed that I was witnessing history in the making. The collapse of Germany was imminent, and I was there. My joy would have been unbounded if I could have only for even a moment have stopped thinking and worrying about my family.

On April 24, 1945, the Americans entered Oberammergau. A seemingly endless procession of tanks rumbled through the village. From the mountains, sporadic shooting by the Germans could be heard. The Americans were on the alert armed with rifles. The general order for the villagers was to stay in the cellars because more shooting might ensue. But Stacha, Zocha, I and the two Russian girls stationed ourselves in front of the restaurant shouting and screaming with joy and waving to the approaching men in the tanks. Some stopped and asked who we were. One tank occupant included a Pole from Chicago and he shouted, "Dowidzenia." By the afternoon Oberammergau was securely in the hands of the Allies. We made available all the food so carefully hidden away by the Königs in the cellar and served scrambled eggs to the soldiers. The war was over! What a feeling. It was difficult to comprehend and to fully appreciate the impact of this so longed-for event.

The next day the Americans gave the "Auslander" workers their day of revenge—they were permitted to take anything they wanted from German homes and from the trains at the station. I sat on the window ledge of our hotel, watching. The last thing in the world I felt like doing was stealing from the Germans. What they did to me could never be paid for by the acquisition of their material things. I had mixed feelings. On the one hand, I was overjoyed and thankful to God. But returning to Poland and worrying about my family was almost more than I could bear. If only I knew that my loved ones were still there. To celebrate this glorious day alone seemed so sad. I kept repeating, "I am alive, the war was over, and the Germans did not kill me. But why am I here when so many, wonderful people are gone?" And then I realized that I did not even strenuously fight or especially wish for my own survival. My life was preserved by others, almost all of them total strangers.

Life in the future, it seemed would be so easy for me. Once the enemy was not lurking at every corner, what could happen to me? I definitely did not need any material things. They did not matter Once I lost my "treasures" in Boryslaw I could not imagine my wanting to be a collector again. As long as I had a bed to sleep in the whole world was open to me. The fact that I was alive and free was surely enough. I saw Zocha bringing six winter coats out of a German house. Even she was not too happy about it now. The German family from whom she took them was the only one in town she knew well. She would not think of entering the house of strangers. She somehow felt ill at ease appropriating the property of "nice" Germans. But she kept repeating to herself, "They are Germans, they are Germans," to justify her actions. I laughed as I looked at her. This seemingly simple, uneducated girl was in reality much more complex than even I suspected. I could not bring myself to tell her, the other girls, or the Königs that I was Jewish, that I found among them a place to hide, and that now I could no longer wait to find my people. But there was no one with whom I could share my feelings.

The Americans were such pleasant happy boys with whom we could laugh. They seemed so totally joyous that it was difficult to believe they fought a devastating war to get here. They behaved like school boys playing ball from the very first hours they arrived in Oberammergau. My English vocabulary consisted of a few words I remembered from the first Berlitz lessons I studied a few years earlier. They hardly understood any German or French, and they all owned those baseball mitts and hard balls. They were watched and admired by all the children in the village. The German Frauleins also visited them with requests for chocolates or cigarettes from the very first day of the American liberation.

A few days later all the foreigners were invited to a party at the American headquarters to celebrate the victory. I did not care for this particular event. I was terribly restless, and unable to decide what I should do next. I wanted to leave quickly so that I might find out what was happening outside of Oberammergau, particularly what had occurred in Eastern Europe. Finally, I told an American officer of Italian descent—thank God I knew some Italian—who was following me throughout the entire evening, that I should like to meet an American who could speak German well, who was in command here, and who preferably was Jewish. He could not think of a Jewish officer at the moment, but he led me to a pleasant looking middle-aged man who spoke German fluently. I explained my situation briefly. The man was leaving for Paris the next day and was not able to do very much for me. He suggested that I leave Oberammergau for Garmisch-Partenkirchen from which place, he thought, displaced persons would be transported to their native countries. We spent quite a few hours talking, but what finally amused him most was the fact that the officer who directed me to him did not know that he was Jewish. I recovered from this initial shock quickly and listened carefully to what he had to say. He felt that I should attempt to emigrate to Palestine instead and did not think that Poland was the place for me. Yes, but how was I to learn about my family?

Two days later I decided to move to Garmisch. Stacha and Zocha and a few Poles sent to Oberammergau after the Warsaw uprising decided to go as well. The two Russian sisters who worked with us had already been picked up by some Russian military men who were looking for Russian slave workers in our part of Germany. The girls were terrified lest they be blamed for allowing themselves to get caught by the Germans for labor. I kissed them and reassured them, only to find out later that all the "slave" workers brought from Germany back to Russia, were sent directly to camps in Siberia for re-education. Stalin's rule had reached its peak of despotism! It turned out that a few of the Russian girls who attached themselves to their foreign lovers and remained in Western Europe were the wise ones.

And so the tower of Babel was rapidly collapsing before my very eyes. More goodbyes issued from the foreign workers, amid promises of reunions, already mixed with the anticipation of meeting those not seen for so long a time. All the new friendships which develop so easily in a foreign country in a time of war and loneliness were abruptly interrupted. These feelings were often more important and intense than those formed in normally happy time, it seemed. I could sense a certain trepidation hidden deep in the hearts of many: how would those who were not seen for years appear now? How much did their loved ones change? I, too, had similar thoughts. I longed to see my parents, aunts, uncles, and cousins, but would I have the courage to face a man I loved years ago? I was not sure. As the future would prove I never was called upon to make such a decision or face these problems.

My mother, my sister and myself in
our home in Boryslaw.

My mother, my sister and myself in
Truskawiec about 1927.

In Venice with my parents and sister
about 1929.

In Porto Rose, Italy (presently Yugoslavia) my sister and myself.

My sister's birthday party in our backyard. She is sitting in the front. I am the fourth from the left.

My sister and myself at a children's birthday party.

My birthday party in the village of Hrebenow. My sister is second from the left. Walterek is on the far right. I am sitting in front.

Our home in Boryslaw about 1930.

My father in our garden in Boryslaw — April 1935.

My sister in our garden. In the
background a wooden tower of an
oil well.

In our backyard with my dear "Kasia."

Privot Gymnasium of King Kazimierz the Great in Boryslaw. I am third in the third row from the left.

Photo from my Polish passport.

With my girl friends in the backyard of our Gymnasium. I am standing first from the left.

I am standing fourth from the left with closed eyes.

My mother's mother, Anna.

My father's mother Maria (in the center) with her two sisters.

My husband "Tom" Polish Army Officer School Warsaw 1937.

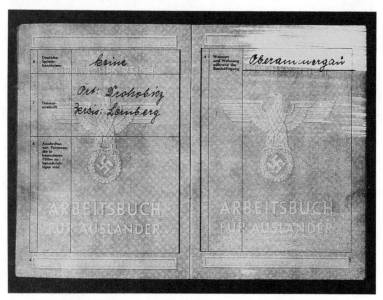

Germany. Work book for foreigners end of January 1943.

# 5

.....

# In Germany After the War

We arrived in Garmisch in a truck that drove straight to a Displaced Persons Camp which was ostensibly organized for the protection of the foreigners, as the Americans claimed. We soon learned its real purpose was to protect the local people from us. Or maybe it served both purposes.

It was a fantastic place in which to find oneself at this particular early state of liberation. All at once we were among people from all over Europe: Italians, Hungarians, Romanians, Czechs, Poles, and Frenchmen. As I was speaking with various persons in their native languages who seemed overjoyed to be there, I noticed a rather mature looking man sitting on a chair in the shadow near a fence, reading a newspaper. I became interested in him only because he did not seem to pay any attention to the wild crowd in the court but continued to read.

Some black soldiers gathered in the middle of the court were the next group to attract my attention. I had never seen so many black people before. Actually, I had previously seen only two. One was a handsome man who was skating in Vienna accompanied by a beautiful white woman. That was years ago. The other one I recalled from my childhood days was at a hotel in Semmering near Vienna, where he was a registered guest. A few of the children loved to sit on his lap in the lobby. Becoming interested, I went over to find out who these black people were. To my surprise they spoke French. They were Moroccan French soldiers. I stood there conversing in French with them, laughing and joking, when the man I noticed earlier with the newspaper walked over to us. He addressed me in French and we started a quick and easy conversation. After half an hour we discovered that we both came from Poland. He was the first Jewish man with whom I became acquainted since the war, but at this particular time I did not know it.

Events were moving quite rapidly, and the greatest one was yet to come. We were all ordered to register, designating our nationality, and as I entered the office to do so for the Polish barrack I heard somebody mention the "Jewish building." I became frantic. I turned to the camp director and whispered, "My God, did somebody say 'Jewish' block?" He looked astonished and asked what I meant. I managed to say that I was Jewish and that I thought that probably there were no other Jewish people here in Germany except for my girlfriend and me. He immediately told me that he was Jewish and invited me to move into the "Jewish quarters." I was in heaven. All the angels were smiling. As it happened I was the first Jewish girl to enter the block—all the others, until then, were men. The next day they had a party for me. Tom, the man with the newspaper, and his friend were also invited. They lived outside the camp in a house that belonged to a German doctor. They brought a bottle of French cognac to the party. A new life began for me.

We sat and talked endlessly, it seemed. When I mentioned that I was from Boryslaw, Tom said he knew a physician in camp who had sisters in that town. It was my Uncle Ludwik. And then it all fitted together so naturally. Tom, a physician, was a survivor of Auschwitz, Dachau, and a few other camps. At Auschwitz he and my Uncle Ludwik worked together for quite a long time. He knew that my Aunt Giza and my little cousin Elzunia were also at Auschwitz, but he did not know what happened to all of them after he was shipped out of Auschwitz. He only heard that my uncle was transferred out of Dachau. Places like Auschwitz and Dachau soon became part of our everyday vocabulary. If Tom survived, I thought, it was also possible that others did.

I lived as if in a trance for the next two days. I was continually attending parties. The Italians celebrated the end of the war in the forenoon, the French in the afternoon, and the Poles in the evening. I decided to explain to my Polish friends why I abandoned them. I confessed first to a Polish man brought from Warsaw to Germany, that I was Jewish. He looked at me in astonishment and quickly added that another member of his group was more familiar with Jewish problems and people. I could see that he felt very uncomfortable. My God, I wondered, were the Jews becoming such a rare species? My faculty for choosing the wrong people was, as usual, below par; but now, I really did not care. The other man was less shocked, but nothing else. No words such as, "I am glad you made it." I did not bother to explain the rest. I no longer worried about it. I was celebrating. I danced as if in a hypnotic state. The Russians were performing their Cossack dances, the Hungarians their Chardash, the Poles, the Polkas—and all the years of war were supposed to be forgotten in those first few carefree days. For me the euphoria lasted only two short ones.

While I was at an evening party Tom entered and asked me to step outside with him for a moment. From his expression I could see that he was not in a gay mood and so could not appreciate the music and the dancing. He asked me directly if I would care to work with him in the hospital that he and a doctor friend of his were establishing for the survivors of the concentration camps who were being brought to Garmisch from the surrounding areas. The American Army authorities had asked them to undertake this project. They needed help because in those first crucial weeks the American doctors were not fully prepared to treat the post-camp diseases and the typhus which usually accompanied them. Tom felt that as a friend of my uncle from Auschwitz he was morally obligated to take care of me. Furthermore, he thought that I had done my share of celebrating the end of the war, and a great deal needed to be accomplished immediately for the other less fortunate survivors. Those few days were among my happiest, but I gladly gave it all up.

Reality with all its attendant horrors intruded upon out lives. The next day the sick were brought in, approximately 150 of them, all found in the surrounding woods, barns or God only knows where. They were the real "Mussulmen" later shown in documentary military movies—emaciated, skeletal men, covered with abscesses, infested with lice, dirty. They were afraid of being approached by German nurses. Male nurses, comprised of healthy survivors, and I would bathe the patients, disinfect them, and generally care for them. I could not eat for the first few days. My stomach was repelled at the sight of food. All I could see and think about were those miserable people. Packages from the Red Cross filled our rooms. All the sick were given their share. This proved to be a terrible mistake. They would voraciously eat cake, sardines, ham and beans all at one time. We soon had more dangerously ill patients than we had treated on the previous day. To add to the effects of starvation and pneumonia, typhus had infected all of them. Tom asked me if I had ever been vaccinated. I lied and said yes. I was afraid of the injection which was administered into the breast. I reasoned that if I had not contracted typhus in Janowska, or when I slept in the same bed with my disease-stricken friend Lusia, I would be safe. For one of the few times in my life I was right—I escaped contagion.

### Tom . . .

I loved to listen to the stories Tom and his friends related about the last days of the war just before they encountered the American tanks. Those were comical tales—not one of us was recalling the horrors and the sad stories. We had all cried enough. Tom, two other doctors and a dentist were in the mountains of Bavaria a day before liberation. They were cold and decided to heat some water. The only container they could find was an empty sardine can. They boiled some water from a stream in the can. The dentist, who was most in need, was the first one to get the water. He drank and kept repeating, "Oh, how good, how good, best drink I ever had, thank you, how good." All of us could imagine how awful water boiled in a sardine can would taste. We laughed. How easy it was to laugh while looking at the still somewhat emaciated dentist who was now drinking a cup of real tea and beaming with the rest of us. Those were our conversations.

Later on "little" Mary became our dentist's assistant. She found us in Garmisch. One day she came to "our" hospital, tearfully said, "I would love to remain here with all of you. I, too, am Jewish. We finally and happily adopted her. With her brown braids pinned around her hair and her winning smile, she was the prettiest addition to the hospital staff.*

The survivors in our group were just marvelous. Quite a few of them maintained that Tom saved their lives in camp, others were just his good friends or patients from Auschwitz or other camps. All of them were constantly in his company and would supply us with everything. Tom worked day and night; and the others, recognizing this, tried to compensate for it by contributing many things which they "organized" around Garmisch. A Hungarian patient of Tom's, who became a shoemaker in camp shortly after liberation, made a pair of brown boots for me, beautifully crafted high ones. Only one who suffered through the war in Europe could appreciate the practical value of this kind of a gift. I did everything but sleep in them, or at least that was what all my friends jokingly claimed.

These people, deeply scarred by war, were always with us and were truly part of us. We entertained a Commission sent by President Truman to report on the condition of the survivors, one of many that visited us from America. We prepared some hors d'oeuvres for them, a "French salad," as Tom called it. He was the cook. Without hesitation he would mix the contents of the American cans we received and used his imagination in preparing meals.

Just before the guests were to arrive at our quarters in the hospital, I went to get some additional cups. While passing through the long corridors I was startled by a Spanish patient, the only one from that country that we had. He was completely naked and kept running from one window to the next, looking through them, and shouting "Seville, Seville" as if he were trying to find his town. He seemed lost and bewildered. However, he was not the only deranged one in the hospital. There surely must have been more, but amazingly enough the state of mind among the majority of our patients alternated from fairly normal to mentally bright. "The human spirit is not easily crushed; the human body can withstand much more punishment than is commonly believed," Tom was always commenting. And I had to agree that it was one of the most salient reasons that some of us survived.

Certain effects of the war, which were sometimes humorous, could be detected in nearly all newly liberated "hefflings" (in-

---

*See Appendix, p. 147.

mates)—They would all carry large suitcases filled with Red Cross cans. They were understandably quite panicky about going hungry again. I remember two doctors who decided to take a trip to Poland to see their old homes. They left with their large, heavy luggage and returned after only one day. They were not strong enough to carry their full bags of cans from one train to another but would not leave without them. Some even insisted on taking them along when they emigrated to the United States.

On the first day I worked in the hospital I fainted at the sight of the open sores on one of the patients being attended by Tom. When I came to, still lying on the floor, I heard him say, "Now you can clean up and boil the instruments," without helping or commiserating with me. I should have realized then what the future held in store for me, but I was quite confident. Regarding Tom, I discovered that my ability to judge people, for once, was still intact. One day Mary asked me, "Why do you spend so much time with Tom? What will you do when he leaves?" Everyone was going somewhere. This startled me. I could not imagine living without him. As it turned out I had no cause for worry. We were married a few weeks later. Since we both worked, we called on the judge at eight in the morning accompanied by "little" Mary and two doctors who acted as our witnesses. I wore the black dress with the white lace collar that I bought in Munich in the "black market" for foreigners. It seemed ages ago, but it was really only within the last few months.

Many of my friends refused to get married without wedding dresses, rings or music. I did not need any of these. All I really wanted was to be with Tom. I found my home away from home with him in a no man's land.

Unexpectedly, I had a wedding reception. Tom's former patients from the camps arranged it for us in the evening. They invited us to a room in the hospital; there was a large table upon which were little sandwiches, cakes and wine. Until this time I had regarded my marriage rather lightly. I wanted to spend all of my time with Tom; and, of course, it was much more convenient to do so if we were married. But now with so many people wishing us well, and happy for us, a new dimension was added. I realized then that my mental state was a serious one. "Was it really for life?" I thought.

After our wedding we spent our free hours walking or riding our bicycles around Garmisch looking at the mountains and admiring the beauty of nature. It still seemed unbelievable that we had survived. To have Tom, who responded in the same way as I did to the beauty around us, to be able to talk with him about books that I had read many years ago, and to be able to read again together the Tuwims poems or "Lalka," or any book we could get, meant that I had finally come home. I could be myself again. Tom saw me as I was, and liked me that way. When I was with him I did not have to make plans. I knew that he would do it for the both of us. I would close my eyes and wonder if these things were really happening to me after all those years.

It was easy to be with Tom. He was an optimist, one who, right after Auschwitz, saw life in a positive light again. He could trust people and felt that they were basically good. I could not believe this so soon after the war. But under Tom's influence I began to accept his thinking slowly, deliberately, realizing that this belief in people's innate "goodness" could make my new life less difficult. I did more or less force myself to trust Tom's judgment till after many years I started to believe in it on my own. Or perhaps not. I am really not sure even now. It was and still is enough for me to think about Janowska in order to doubt any normal conceptions of human nature. At times it seems that I never really left Janowska, and probably would not want to leave it ever again. If I had ever had the choice of a different life, would I have done it? No, I think not. If the events I survived have become an integral part of my life, then I accept experiencing them personally. I leave the illusions to others.

### The News from Home

One day we were swimming in a lake in Feldafing, Tom, "little" Mary, myself and a few friends. We were all good swimmers and crossed the lake to the other side. We stopped briefly at a cottage of one of Tom's patients. Tom and I soon left for the hospital where we were then stationed. After a while Mary came running in. She looked at me and tearfully embraced me. "Ludka, she said, your father is alive." My first reaction was, "My father, what do you mean my father, and what about my mother?" And then she told me the whole story. After Tom and I left the cottage, one of the men who was visiting there, told Mary, "—Interesting, how this girl who was just here reminds me so much of Ludka of Boryslaw," to which Mary replied, "She is Ludka." The young man told her that he had just come from Poland and heard that my father was once again Director of the Polish oil industry. He did not hear anyone speak about my mother. Tom and I ran to the cottage to learn all the details, but there was little else that the man could tell us. He was returning to Poland on the next day but refused to take me with him. I wanted so desperately to go. Women who crossed the border were still being raped by the Russians on the east-west German border which we would have to cross to get into Poland. I had to be satisfied with giving him a letter to my parents written by Tom and myself and wet with my tears. The young man promised to deliver it personally and to bring us an answer in about two weeks. I did not know how I would survive while waiting. Many thoughts kept running through my mind, but the predominant one was the uncertain feeling about my mother. Was she there with my father? The time passed more rapidly than I imagined. Shortly after, Tom learned that his younger sister had survived and was now in Bergen-Belsen, a concentration camp now occupied by the English army. As Tom's patients were then being transferred to other hospitals, we decided to find her immediately and to return in two weeks to meet with the man from Poland.

The train from Munich was scheduled to depart sometime in the late afternoon, but no one knew exactly when, since no time tables were available as yet. We had to wait for a train travelling in the direction of our destination, to arrive. At midnight I stretched out on my suitcase and slept until morning. For once being short proved to be a boon. Not until a train for Kassel arrived the following day did we realize that we would have to ride on top of the coal car. It was really much more comfortable than we thought it would be, as coal could be shifted around and was firm enough to lend support to the body. The big surprise lay ahead when, after spending the night on the coal bed, we arrived in Wirtzburg in the early morning only to discover that we all looked as if we had fallen out of a chimney. Our party consisted of Tom, myself and two men who also traveled to Bergen-Belsen in search of their wives. On the second day we reached Kassel, and until then I had never fully appreciated the enormous extent of the devastation of German towns. We walked on piles of rubble for many kilometers before we found a house that was inhabitable. One member of our group was looking for a family in Kassel, and we all accompanied him. But it was soon became obvious that no one would be found in this town. On the way back to the station we came upon an apple tree covered with red fruit. From a nearby shack a woman appeared and told us to pick some. Somehow the beautiful tree made the whole scene even sadder.

Bergen-Belsen, located not far from Bremen, was a large concentration camp swarming with women, now with smiling faces, nicely dressed, well groomed and under the protection of the English. The newly built graveyards of thousands of women was the sole and mute witness to the murders perpetrated by the Germans and the terrible typhus disease which infected the inmates of the camp at the end of the war. But as it happened everywhere else, those who survived were emerging, all young and eager and full of renewed hope.

It was not too difficult to find Irena, Tom's beautiful sister. She was well known there. We spent nights talking with her and with the other women. Those horror stories, upon which no one wanted to dwell, were mentioned only briefly. I knew Irena's story. She was a teenager when she married a pathologist during the first year of the war. Shortly after, the whole family, Irena, her husband, Tom, his wife, a dentist, and their mother were sent to Auschwitz. Their mother was condemned to the gas chamber right after they arrived. Tom's wife and Irena's husband volunteered for death after their first month in camp. They simply could not cope with the conditions there, and both capitulated early. Now Tom and Irena were together crying, laughing and planning their future. Their uncle, a colonel in the American army, was in command of the port of Bremen but left for the United States before he learned that Irena and Tom had survived. He now asked a friend of his stationed in Bremen to contact Irena, which he did. We all decided then to visit the colonel in Bremen.

Upon our arrival in this large port city, still partially in shambles, Irena and Tom went to look for their uncle and left me to guard the suitcases in a little park. I waited for a while and then became terribly impatient. I was here in Bremen with the Baltic Sea so near. I just had to see it. I took the suitcases to a nearby drugstore and asked the pharmacist to keep an eye on them so I could get to the port. I did not realize that the city was not located directly on the sea. In my eagerness I did not ask how far it was. After walking for more than an hour I turned back, very disappointed. It was yet another hour before I returned, jumping through and over rubble. I got back to the park, half dead. Irena and Tom did not share my enthusiasm for the sea, not at this time. They were afraid that I had disappeared. For years Tom kept repeating the story of my failed expedition in search of a port. We left town on the next day with many gifts from the kind American colonel. He presented all of us with a watch, our first one after the war! Irena decided to return to our place near Munich. The same adventure we previously experienced on an open coal train brought us back to the place from which we started.

A few days later the young man arrived from Poland with a letter from both of my parents. I did not have to open it to know. Marian told me right at the start how he found my parents in Krakow, how they kissed and embraced him, how eager they were to know everything about me, how I looked, if I was healthy, and who was Tom! Together, there in the Krakow apartment with my parents, was Oleś—Oh God, at least I knew that right away. And then when everybody left I opened their letter and read it with tears streaming down my face. I was sitting there holding a communication written by my mother and father after a war which the three of us survived. "God in heaven, you were with us. Thank you." Soon I was to find out the rest—the fate of our entire family. From their letter, so full of love and happiness, I slowly passed to the tear-stained pages. From our dearest, it was only little Oles, my Aunt Judith, her husband Jack, and my mother's brother Ludwik who were still alive. Later, to the list of survivors, was added Oles' father, my Uncle Lonek, who was liberated in the concentration camp at Gross-Rosen. He was too sick for months to be able to contact the family.

And this was how it all happened. In 1944, months before the Russians entered our town, it was quite apparent that the Germans were preparing a mass "Selection" to eliminate all those who were unable to work, followed by a deportation of all those remaining. When the day came to move within the camp, my grandfather did not realize that my grandmother and he with the other elders were to be taken to their death. He dressed neatly in his best suit and white shirt and prepared to go to camp. My parents told him that grandmother and he were going into hiding in a basement especially prepared for them. My grandmother's cousin and his wife were also there along with a younger maid who was to take care of all of them. My parents left a box with them containing gold coins for their use in an emergency. They all kissed and embraced, my mother wrote, knowing full well that this would be the last time they would see each other. In early March of 1944, just before the final deportation of all Jews from Drohobycz, my parents were approached by a former employee of my father's who asked them to come to her hiding place in the attic. This courageous Polish woman was very grateful to my father, remembering how he had arranged for her to get wood for a house that she built shortly before the war. She also claimed that she was encouraged by members of the Polish underground who wanted to save some Jews. At this time little Oleś was already in hiding. He stayed with a decent Ukrainian family, a member of which had been an employee in my uncle's oil wells. They cared for Oleś and treated him as if he belonged to them. Their daughters taught him to read and write. At one time he had helped to distribute ammunition to the Ukrainian partisans. The same people also agreed to hide my Aunt Giza, Oleś's mother, but she was reluctant to go, afraid that her presence might endanger her small son. She finally agreed to be hidden, but she was a day late. She was sent to Auschwitz with my fourteen year old cousin Elzunia, her niece, whose mother, Ila, was already dead. She was "selected" for an earlier random deportation. Elzunia's father was taken to the Ravensbruck camp where he died before the Americans arrived. My Uncle Joseph, the older brother of my father, died in Auschwitz.

My Aunt Giza and Elzunia remained in Auschwitz almost until the arrival of the Russians. At this time the Germans took some of the women to Stuthoff, on the Baltic, where twenty-five thousand of them were forced into the sea. Those who swam out were shot at by the SS. As related by a woman who escaped, Elzunia was already very ill on the way to Stuthoff. She suffered from an ear infection and was running a high fever. Giza was trying to carry her. Elzunia was shot along the way by a German before she reached the Baltic.

As further described by my mother, her parents were discovered in their hiding place by the Gestapo. Shortly afterwards my Aunt Judith found an inscription on the wall of the deportation center which read, "After long suffering we are finally going to our death."

It was signed by my grandmother. My grandparents did not take the poison they carried with them. Their religion forbade them to take their own lives. They gave it away, a survivor recalled.

Walterek and Zosia perished earlier than the others. My parents received two letters from Walterek.* In the first he informed us that Zosia was dead and that he was dying from starvation. He asked my parents for help. They sent money and a package to him through a Polish worker and learned of Zosia's fate from a survivor. She was well liked by the Germans at her place of employment. She and four other workers were the last remaining Jews in Lwow, outside of Janowska camp. Since other transports no longer left, all four were burned alive in a building. This is what the survivor told my mother. No one else remained to confirm the story.

Walter was finally at Janowska. My parents once more sent him a package and a letter. He took the letter with him to the washroom where he was caught reading it by an SS man who beat him to death. I was able to visualize this terrible scene so well. I always prayed that no one dear to me would come there when I was present—and thanked God for sparing me that eventuality. I suppose that I did not pray enough, because my beloved Walterek was not saved.

When my mother wrote the letter Judith and Jack were already in Paris. Throughout the last phase of the war they were both in hiding on a farm. My uncle met the farmer while working in Drohobycz, and when the final deportation was near in late March of 1944, he mentioned to the owner that he had a few gold dollars which he would gladly offer for a safe place to hide. The man suggested that he and Judith stay in his barn. They remained there for a few weeks, but as all the other Jews were still in camp and had not as yet been deported, they too decided to return. As they were approaching their destination on April 14, they saw lines of SS men and trucks surrounding the entire camp. They quickly retreated to their hiding place.**

One more of our dear ones survived, my Uncle Ludwik. During one of the "selections" he worked in the hospital and was assured that his family was safe. He learned, too late, that his wife and only

---

*See Appendix, p. 138.
**See Appendix, pp. 144-147.

daughter, thirteen year old Rysienka, had been deported. He was sent to Auschwitz much later, as a political prisoner, where he was beaten mercilessly to make him confess all of his activities. Later he shared a bunker with Tom. The world was becoming very small. Right after the war Ludwik married a wonderful woman who was with him in Auschwitz, and who Tom also met in camp. From his detailed description I got to know my new Aunt Roma long before I finally met her. From Tom's observations as well, I learned a great deal about Roma's cousin, David, and his wife, Saba, all former inmates of Auschwitz. They became our dear and long lasting friends, our closest family.

My mother and father never explained how they spent five months with eleven other people in one small attic, how much food they had, or what sanitary conditions were available. I could not bring myself to ask. I have my parents' pictures after they left their shelter. They speak for themselves. I also have the two spoons and forks they used while there. Liberated by the Russians on August 6, 1944, my parents went immediately to pick up Oleś and met Judith and Jack. No one else was there. Someone suggested that my parents move back to our house. They would not hear of the idea, but they did go to take a look at it. The German owner had built a swimming pool and a tennis court where our garden used to be. A few weeks later my parents, and what was left of our family, moved to Krakow. My father once again became a Director in the Polish oil industry, now, of course, much smaller. Judith and Jack went to Paris, and Oleś finally was enrolled in a normal school. Then, one day, he returned home and said that he would never attend school again.* A child had called him ". . . Jew. . . ." At this time my parents learned the Oles' father, Lonek, survived Gross-Rosen and was now in Berlin. They both decided that Oleś should join his father in Berlin and from there migrate to Palestine.

I read the letter over and over again, numbed with disbelief. I could not comprehend or accept its contents as valid, not then, and not now. In the letter my parents wrote that now, learning that I was alive and in Germany, they would join Tom and me and hoped that together we would emigrate to the United States.

Prior to my parents' arrival, Tom's father, Samuel, came to visit. We knew for some time that he had spent the war time in Siberia.

---

*See Appendix, p. 142.

He had been sent there in 1939. He survived and was back in Poland and planned to visit us on his way to America.

My father-in-law's arrival affected the entire hospital. Tom was the Director then. Samuel was an exceptionally handsome man, over six feet tall, slim and strong. He looked much healthier and more alert than any one of the survivors of the German camps. He was wearing the same shoes he had on in 1939, repaired many times, of course. The strength and self-assurance of this man was tremendous. He could have been a great leader in Europe or in any other place in the world, given the opportunity. After a few days he left for Paris and from there, on to New York.

During the two years we stayed in Germany, Tom became Medical Director of Gauting, a thousand bed hospital, and then was named Administrative Director at Bad Wörrishofen where our daughter was eventually born. Both hospitals were established by the UNRRA. Throughout this time the attitude of the German physicians toward Tom was a source of amusement to us. The German doctors would hold the doors open for him as he walked from room to room. At least three of them would rush to help him put on his coat. They would never sit down before he did. They would address me as, "Gnadige Frau Chief Doctor." Bestowing upon me Tom's complete title. This made me wonder later on why I ever bothered to get my own doctorate after this treatment. It was also offensive to me. I looked at these young and middle-aged doctors fawning and generally behaving like servants, alternating so easily from one extreme to another. It was probably nothing more than the routine German Army behaviour toward a senior officer. I would have much preferred to encounter their hostility. There we were, victors of the moment, while they were scraping before us. This was yet another historic moment, temporary perhaps, but nevertheless so very typical.

On another occasion one of the doctors told me that while visiting one of the concentration camps during the war, he would throw his cigarette butts on the floor for the inmates to find. I looked at him. I could painfully visualize the whole scene. I would see him, ten feet tall, and the inmates crowding and pushing to pick up the butts. And now he was sitting here in my living room, and I was smiling politely at him, not even interested in knowing about which camp he was talking, lest I break down. I knew that Tom would arrive shortly, and that this man would jump up and greet him with all his military agility, and again the gratuitous smiles and small talk would continue. I felt ill, but this was a new phase in our lives. Tom and the German doctors were performing the same duties— trying their utmost to bring the camp survivors back to health.

One of the foreign physicians employed a German secretary whose father lived in Warsaw during the war who she often visited. I looked at the three fur coats she wore during the first winter after the war, and wondered. Then there was a Joint Distribution Committee representative who brought shoes from America for the patients. He made sure that his Fraulein got the first pick. I finally had to admit that Tom was right—life was moving on and I could spend it in many different ways. The choice of course should have been mine. But as it turned out it was really Tom's. We were definitely making progress.

### My Parents Arrive

Our affidavits for the trip to the United States arrived, and we were required to appear for examinations in Munich. Of course we took our baby, whom I still nursed, with us. I knew that my parents were already in Berlin, separated from us only by the Russian zone. When and how they would get to us I did not know. I just hoped they would come before we left for the States in November.

I was walking in the court of the camp ground where we stayed in Munich when I heard some one call my name, Ludeczka, just as it was at home. I knew immediately that it was my mother. There she stood, dressed in a gray suit and white silk blouse, her hair beautifully set, my dearest one as lovely as ever. She knew that she was coming to see me after all those years, to meet Tom and the baby, and she wanted to look her best. Otherwise what would Tom and his friends think of me? Into what kind of a family would Tom think he had married? I knew my dear mother, I knew her so well. Words were not needed for communication between us. All the tears, fears, and tragedies she suffered through all those years were buried deep in her heart for none to ever know. The world was moving and she right along with it.

We were a family once again where conventions mattered, where a physician has his place, a doctor's wife her social standing, a

mother-in-law her very own role to play. Only we were not back in
Boryslaw on Legionow 20, but in a displaced persons camp in
Munich. However, that did not really matter.

Then I found myself standing in front of my father. I noticed
that his blue eyes were moist when he kissed and embraced the
baby and me. So that is what it basically was—we survived. I looked
at them, and at once we knew what we were all thinking about.
Where were all the others? But the unspoken query lasted only a
second. Arrangements had to be made for my parents' sleeping
accommodations, we had to find Tom, and the baby had to be fed.

At night while I was lying in bed, too excited to fall asleep, I kept
thinking of how little my parents had changed. It was nearly two
years since the war ended. They had time to recuperate physically.
The only thing that struck me was the difference in the expression
in my mother's eyes. It was not the one I remembered from childhood, then so bouyant and full of life. Now there was a deep sadness that could be detected even when my mother laughed. It was
more evident in my father's eyes. Only when they looked at my
baby would the old spirit return, but only for a moment.

We hardly spoke about our years of separation, and we never sat
down to talk and cry about the pain it engendered. Sometimes one
word would trigger some reminiscences. I never asked how they
managed to survive in the attic, although it bothers me even now
when I think about it. Instead, my mother would recall how she
found Oleś, and how he would say, "Do not always say that one is
not supposed to do this or that—rather tell me what I should do."
He remembered so much from home, but not everything, and too
much was probably expected of him. Once my mother told me
how Elzunia failed to greet the Oberrsturmfuhrer during the
"Appel" [roll call] in camp the day after her mother died, and how
offended he was. And that is what prompted the telling of my
mother's own story which took some unusual turns after we last
parted in Lwow in 1943.

After my mother, who was quite sick, was brought back to my
father in Drohobycz, she had no job and was in danger of deportation momentarily. She did not have the required letter "R"
which signified a "needed" worker.* After a few days had passed,
my Uncle Leon came running in to her room and told her that the

---

*See Appendix, pp. 135-136.

secretary of the SS man, Hechtsmann, in charge of the work camp they were in, took sick. He suggested that she should apply for this job. At first, my mother was terrified—she could not type or take notes and hadn't worked at all for twenty-five years since she met and married my father. But then, after my uncle pointed out that getting this job could save not only her life but that of other members of the family, she agreed. Trembling, and almost paralyzed with fear, as she described it, she went to the SS office and was hired at once. She started to take dictation, typed it, and within a few hours her old skills returned. She was able to satisfactorily perform her secretarial duties.

After she was employed there for a few weeks, her sister, Judith, and her husband, Jack, were sent to prison to await deportation. When my mother learned about this, she asked her boss for help. He released them immediately. That was how she saved their lives.* Later when my aunt, Ila, was seized, my mother tried again, but this time Hechtsmann refused to intercede. There was another worker who together with my mother begged him to free her own relatives; even for the two of them, he would not intervene. All her tears were in vain. Late on this day when my parents went to the prison to see Ila, she told them she was not scared. These were the only words she kept repeating, but she eventually took cyanide. A survivor confirmed that this was how my always happy aunt, the one who was the least prepared to suffer, ended her life. It was on the morning of the next day that her daughter Elzunia did not greet the Obersturmfuhrer at "Appel." My mother's voice was so completely flat and colorless when she recounted it, her face drained and ashen. I wanted to know, but did not have the courage or strength to ask, how Ila looked when my parents saw her last, and for how long they were allowed to visit with her. I tried to picture this scene so many times, but I would only envision Ila standing as if in a glass coffin separated from all that she loved so dearly.

My mother recalled once more how her father dressed in a clean white shirt and his best suit to accompany them to camp, and they were unable to take him. This was the last time she saw him and her mother. She just mentioned Zosia and Walterek, but those were her thoughts and with them a sadness was reflected in her

---

*See Appendix—Judith's Story, pp. 145-147.

eyes. It was from my mother that I also learned of Alma's fate. She
was caught in Zakopane near Krakow, transported to Auschwitz
and according to some died in Stuthoff by drowning in the Baltic
Sea. But this would not have been like Alma, I thought. She was
quite a competent, professional swimmer. Unless she was shot she
would have been able to swim to safety.

My father was already under pressure thinking about how he
would earn a living in the United States. What would the new life
bring him, away from his lifelong responsibilities and without his
high executive standing? I knew that his emigration to the States
frightened him, or maybe I only thought so because it scared me. I
could not picture my life in the States, among all those carefree
people who had little or no idea of how we suffered. I thought of
them all as happy-go-lucky as the young GI's I met throughout
Germany. With others who lived through our hell, words were not
needed, we just looked at each other and felt a mutual bond of
understanding.

I also worried about how I would feel being so poor in an affluent
society where everyone else was purportedly quite wealthy. That's
exactly what I thought—a country of millionaires! And where
would I take my baby for a walk in New York with all its crowds
and skyscrapers? I worried even after we received the letter from
Tom's Uncle Bill, a most wonderful and reassuring one.

I also knew that William, a cousin of my father's who went to the
States in the summer of 1939 to visit the World's Fair and was
unable to return to Europe, offered to secure an apartment for us.
His wife, Janka, was killed in Warsaw while living there with Aryan
papers. It was for her that I looked, among others, in those fright-
ful hours in Warsaw in May of 1943. Their son Richard, who was
cared for by their maid in the village in which she lived, was expected
to join William shortly. I knew my cousin would be happy to see
us, but nothing seemed to allay my anxieties. I would have given
almost anything to avoid going to the States, but Tom's family was
already there—his father, his sister, Irena, and of course his sister,
Roda, and her husband. It would have been unconscionable for us
not to join them, but I still dreaded it. Frankly I was afraid.

I did not remember my cousin William too well but I recalled his
wife, Janka, through one small incident which occurred, it seemed
like, ages ago. She was one of the guests who arrived from Lwow

for the wedding of my Aunt Giza and Uncle Lonek which took place in our house. After long hours of festivities all the guests departed. As my parents, Judith—who remained—Doneczka and I dropped dog-tired on the lounge chairs and couch, we heard the bell ring. Wearily one of us ran to open the door and there was Janka, all smiles. She came back to see how happy we were that the wedding finally came to an end, and that every one left. We laughed for quite a while and admired her down-to-earth sense of humor.

William readied the apartment we were to occupy, I assumed, for her. She had everything to live for but was the only one of my father's family who perished. Destiny again!

Tom's sister, Roda, and her husband, Steven, an ophthamologist, arrived in the United States in 1937. Steven was now in Europe with the American army.

I always liked the story of how Roda found out that Tom had survived. She was at work when a friend called to tell her that she saw Tom's picture in a newspaper. A few weeks earlier, a delegation from President Truman had come to inspect the hospital where Tom served as the physician in charge, and they took both our pictures. By coincidence the delegation was from Texas, and the picture was published in the local newspaper. From that time onward the cigarettes we received from Roda were one of the main sources of our well being. Her marvelous letters were very encouraging, but still not persuasive enough to make me enthusiastic about emigrating to the States.

### On the Way to the USA: The Camp in Bremen Haffen

On our way to the United States at the end of November, 1946, we spent two months in Bremen while waiting for the ship, which, because of the coal strike, was detained in the States. There, among a large group of other survivors, we had plenty of leisure time to think, observe, and discuss how the war affected us, who we are now, and what really did happen. We found precious few answers.

It was in our first hospital in Garmisch where we observed the deteriorating effects of the war on people. They were usually consistent with the age of the person at the onset of the war. Those who were already in their mid-twenties and older, whose characters were fully developed, who experienced enough of normal living and those who maintained certain established principles, emerged virtually unchanged. They were polite to others and routinely accepted pre-war values and standards. The most affected were the few children who survived. They had not as yet established a permanent canon of beliefs and standards. It was difficult enough to try to keep them in line in our hospital for vaccinations. They would always push the others in front of them to be first and acted as if their very lives depended on it. Throughout their brief existences they were forced to fight like little animals to survive, and that was all they knew.

Later, I was amazed to find how little impact the war had on my parents. They maintained their pre-war values, gentleness and morality as if untouched by the cruelties they bore and witnessed. They were both strong individuals with an abundance of inner dignity. I admired my father from the time I was a child, but during the war and after, it was my mother who became for me the epitome of strength and stability. My parents could not understand why, at this stage, I could not approach and live my life as they had taught me. They could not accept the fact that I was too young when the war started to establish my entire life on their principles and not be touched and influenced by what I had experienced since. Tom, who was in his late twenties when his life was so tragically disrupted, came through it all virtually unchanged in spite of the suffering. That was how every one of us, each in a different way, faced the future and the new life for better or worse.

Again and again we would think about the war, our experiences and those of others. We would ask ourselves if we could have foreseen the German plan that doomed every one of us to death, would we have from the beginning started to kill, run, even fight with our bare hands? Maybe, but we never thought about mass killings. We could never have dreamed about a plan so barbaric simply because throughout modern history no diabolic plan of this magnitude was ever perpetrated. To be sure, murders were committed, inhumane torturing took place, but never before was there such a meticulously planned genocide as the one organized and implemented by Hitler and Himmler. We were living in the twentieth century, and somehow people were expected to act in accordance with the humanitarian principles of decency, as outlined by the Geneva Convention and religious teachings.

Even more inexplicable was the fact that these atrocities were being committed by people whose culture the world so greatly admired. Who could ever believe that there would be people who could plan to exterminate babies, women, and indeed a whole race, or that the German people would sanction and hail those who performed these barbarities.

Who could ever have dreamed that this bestiality would be embraced so quickly by other European nations. After the last deportation in a town not far from ours, a baby was left in an empty house, as often happened. It was brought to the attention of the SS man in charge of the action. He had probably seen enough blood already or was simply too tired to act himself. He took a small oriental rug from the house in which the baby was found, placed the infant on it, and announced that whoever killed the baby could have the rug. The tenseness, hate, resentment, feelings of shame, guilt and superiority always thrived among the onlookers as well as the Germans after every deportation. A middle-aged plain looking woman picked up the baby and with one strong swing, crushed its little body on the ground, picked up the rug and walked away. How many of us would have been able to commit the brutal murders of which the Germans were capable. Theirs was the master plan—no one wishes to take that "glory" away from them. May it never be forgotten as long as people live.

But then how was it possible that they were able to poison others so easily? Who, for example, were the Ukrainians who followed them so determinedly? Here the question was readily answered by my father who defended them in many discussions. They were largely an uneducated group, badly treated for centuries, to whom "culture" was totally alien as it was to aborigines, except of course for those few intelligent Ukrainians who proved to be as idealistic and as giving of themselves as any chosen people in the full meaning of the word. Who then were the Estonian and Latvian troops whom we had never seen before, and who the SS was able to enroll as helpers in the camps? And who were the others who witnessed the cruelties and remained indifferent to all the indignities, again with so few exceptions? Who really were those people? What made them act this way? Where was the hope for humanity? Are we any better? How many of us would sacrifice our lives for others? Or did this quality cease to be the dominant characteristic of the human race?

The Jewish policemen were also known for their lack of compassion towards their fellow Jews. If the lives of their own wives, husbands or children were in danger, all the others would be sacrificed. That was how they operated and how they earned their awful reputation. I always felt that when they entered my room in Lwow one night, looking for my friend Lusia, and found me, and very likely noticed my mother hidden under the covers, they did not arrest us because their own families were not at risk.

Of course, some of the Jews were rank opportunists, people without scruples and with no soul. One of these was a cook in Janowska. He was killed by the inmates after they learned that he was selling food for money and diamonds while the rest were starving. Unfortunately there were quite a few like him.

And what about all of us who were only trying to survive? Weren't we fit to live? Would it have been more glorious for us to die as martyrs? Each of us had only one life to live, one which another human was trying to take away. It was like a one sided fight on a battlefield, because we did not have the guns to resist. We couldn't use our bare hands against the enemies' tanks and guns. We had no organization. We were alone. And we were doomed.

While in Janowska a few men, an architect, and other professionals with whom we would meet in the office when they reported to Gebauer, mentioned that they were working out some plans. They never did tell me exactly what kind. It was the end of 1941. At the beginning of 1942, the realization of all our hopes and dreams was focused on the Americans, and President Roosevelt was our god. We continually talked about the Americans in our office and wondered when they would send somebody to help us organize, to supply ammunition, or even if and when they would let us know that they were aware of us here in Janowska. The last matter of recognition was what we really wanted most of all. As a group we could not have accomplished anything in the hostile world of the local population. Individually we could not escape because for every one who succeeded a hostage would be shot. There was no one to suggest a different way. I was always ready for a big adventure. I wanted desperately to become a courier, to steal in and out of camp innumerable times; if only I was enlisted to do this important job. Alma and others could have done well. But there was no one to talk with, no one to ask for advice. Each of us was faced with his or her own individual problems. When I was hungry, I did not believe I was incapable of even thinking about it at all. I just longed for a larger piece of bread.

Soon after the war a nice American nurse who I met at a party told me that she was grateful not to have been in Europe during the war because she always thought of herself as becoming a heroine and would have been afraid to find out that under fire she really wasn't. First, I laughed, but then I kept thinking about her fears. What was I doing during the entire war? Trying to save myself. Just because someone decided that I was not fit to live, I spent four long years striving to survive. Truth to tell, I never really cared. But to be heroic?

I never met any heroes or heroines, I thought at first. Then it occurred to me that in a valid way my father could be called one for refusing to run so as not to abandon the other members of our family. Or similarly, my aunt and uncle not hiding with Oles' lest they endanger his life by their presence. Or perhaps the boy in Janowska whose father, a prominent member of the Judenrat who had influenced Gebauer to set him free, only to have the boy insist on staying and dying with the others.

Inmates who were in camp with Tom often spoke about how, at great personal risk, he helped others; but Tom never mentioned this.

Who else? I would have to think a great deal. Certainly, I was no heroine. I did not even think of myself as a good person. Perhaps if I had been different, I would have behaved otherwise, I would have done more for others, I might even have tried the impossible. But I didn't.

I also recall that before the German occupation we had friends, acquaintances, and enemies. That's how we categorized people. During the war it was "Ukrainian," "Jew," "German." It was as simple as that. As a group, the Ukrainians were quite dangerous because they could somehow recognize a Jew, while the Germans could not. Still there were some good Ukrainians to whom a number of Jews owed their lives, including, in several instances, myself. When one spoke of these, the characterization would be "a decent Ukrainian" and that was all that needed to be said.

Some Poles also suffered a great deal, and some, of course, more than others. As a group they were not dangerous but would not help either. Among these people were those who expected to get paid for what they did or for not denouncing. Others would hide Jews, expecting no payoff, out of friendship and compassion for other human beings. That was how my parents were saved. There was no justification for people who denounced us, but, on the other hand, there was no condemnation for those who refused to hide us either, as hiding Jews subjected the hider to the same fate as the one hidden. So much more could have been done, but so very few even tried.

A Polish woman came to see my mother of her own volition. She was the wife of a magazine supervisor who worked for the same company as did my father. She offered to store away some of our valuables for us. By this time my mother had so very little left. Still, whatever we possessed, and I now still treasure, was safely kept by this most thoughtful and generous woman. My grandparents must have had a few true friends. After the war, and long after they were killed, two of their suitcases were returned to us. Some of my photographs, including those of my sister and parents, my most prized treasures, were hidden in this luggage. Included also were my grandmother's trousseau linens which she had personally embroidered. She had not used them for years, but it must have meant a great deal to her to decide to leave them for safekeeping with a friend hoping that after the war her cherished belongings would be returned to her. Among my grandmother's belongings were the first hair locks cut from her little boys' heads—the same from my father, and uncles Joseph and Lonek. Those were the precious things with which grandmother would not part. She was a collector. When all the children would visit her, she would show us the large chest in which she stored all the treasures she had accumulated. There were her boys' first pairs of shoes, first white suits, and memorabilia that had previously belonged to her parents. I wondered who broke apart this chest, and angered at finding nothing of value to the looter, threw it all into the garbage—my grandmother's collection of a lifetime. None of us wanted to safeguard "riches" for the post war period, but only a few precious mementos.

One thing was certain, without some help from others, none of us in Bremen waiting for the ship bound for the United States, would have survived. The names of those Poles, Ukrainians and Germans who helped us have not been recorded, but they did exist, and they gave some hope and solace to mankind and particularly to me. To a degree they enabled me to care and love again.

In my own thoughts I always seemed to contradict myself. I would become argumentative with those with whom I discussed various problems. If some praised the Poles or Ukrainians, I would object; when others condemned them I would extol those helpful ones. And that approach was true in any of my discussions about the Germans.

But these mental exercises were to the be all and the end all of my own speculations, for whatever they were worth. Other people's debates would provoke new anxieties. There was the assumption on the part of psychologists that we survivors possessed a feeling of guilt. I always wondered how they reached such a conclusion. I definitely felt elated about the survival of those I knew. Unfortunately there were so few. As for myself, I never harbored any guilt after the war. On the contrary, I considered my survival my own small private victory over the Nazis. But it really was not personal. I did not try too aggressively. It was due mostly to the few real "human" beings who fortuitously crossed my path at just the right time. It was their triumph more than it was mine. But then the psychologists would say, "You are too close to the problem, you are too involved, so how can you really know?" I realized too that the sociologists also were doing their best to explain situations which were new, with little success.

I personally felt that these were not the major issues, that there were other more general ones concerning all of mankind, not survivors exclusively. It became obvious to me, when I thought about the ghettos and camps, that our culture was lacking that certain moral fibre that might have prevented the horrors we suffered. We were the ones who had lived through the tragedy, and no one else would either believe it or even care to think about it. It became clear to me, at least, that there are more things wrong with our civilization than we realize. Somehow, it seemed to me, we were all guilty. This conviction I am certain will always remain with me.

# 6

· · · · ·

# Epilogue: America

We arrived in New York on January 13, 1947. It was a rainy day. When we approached the city from afar, we could see the Statue of Liberty through a dense fog, a sight I never was too anxious to see. We are all standing on the deck of the ship "Ernie Pyle." This was to be its last voyage.

From the movies I saw and the books I read, I learned how the refugees reacted when they first caught sight of the Statue of Liberty in New York harbor at the end of a long journey. Their elation was unbounded. Not me, I always thought. But there I was standing on the deck, all smiles, and with a heart filled with joy and hope. So it was also happening to me—the feeling of excitement, and anticipation. Here I was experiencing the same emotions so singular among other refugees. I gazed at the skyscrapers barely visible through the mist, their windows reflecting a golden glow. This sight was beautiful. More magnificent than anything I had ever seen before. I was seeing all this with my seven-month-old baby and my husband, new refugees in a new land.

My luggage consisted of a gray wooden box, two large cardboard suitcases, and a baby carriage. Our total assets on arrival were eight dollars; one dollar that Tom was given as a good luck piece by our American nurse, and seven dollars that he won in a bridge game on the ship. He was an excellent card player. I wore my sister's gray suit; the one I had on when I arrived in Oberammergau. It was the only clothing I had, and, of course, it was also my best. Just before debarking and while waiting in the long line, I thought for a brief moment that I would rather have remained in the country in which I was born—only I never really had a country. It was here that I had to replant my roots.

There were so many things I had not foreseen. For instance, I could not envision that after the first two painfully difficult years, we would do well financially. I also never realized that I would remain a "foreigner" or "refugee" or "newcomer" for the rest of my life. It bothered me during those first years that I was not able to accurately guess, while talking with people, their background or degree of education. Everyone spoke English perfectly, except me! I never knew about the many other problems which I was supposed to experience as an immigrant, and my children as well, as first generation Americans, until I enrolled for my first course in Sociology. If I had read, while in Europe, the chapter on "Emigrants to America" from the required text, I definitely would not have dared to come to this new country. I was fortunate not to have studied that discouraging chapter first.

I was both surprised and upset by the American approach to "Stalinism." They really had no idea what "Stalinism" meant. When we came to the United States in 1947, the consensus sympathies were pro-Russian, especially among the intellectuals. No one here knew how dangerous it was to live under Stalin's despotic rule. When I tried to explain I would hear the same cliché, "You were too close to the situation to see things clearly . . ." The people who would argue with me were good, idealistic human beings, the first ones who in all likelihood would have been unable to survive under Stalin's rule. But they were just unaware of all the circumstances. They believed in Marxism only theoretically but were ignorant of its failed implementation. It was almost unbelievable to me that the tyrant's atrocities were virtually unknown, even to scholars.

They also had their own theory about why we emigrated— we came here for material reasons. If they only knew how little materialism meant to us. All that we ever wanted was to be able to speak and express our opinions freely, and to raise our children in a country they would be proud to call theirs.

My father always thought that Americans were like children, so completely politically naive. When the unfortunate McCarthy phenomenon burst upon the scene, he was greatly worried. He was no longer among us to witness the responsible adult development of the American youth in the sixties. He would have truly appreciated this promising progress.

Tom and I returned to Germany during the mid-sixties. We went back, as so many survivors did, to places we had known earlier. We returned to where Tom saw the first American soldiers, Bad Worishoffen and Oberammergau. Once while in a restaurant in Innsbruck I was sure that I recognized a Gestapo man sitting two tables away, only to discover, upon a closer look, that he was a French tourist visiting here with his family. Then we returned to Poland. When I arrived in Warsaw, I was not sure that I would be able to deplane. But I did, and we toured the entire city and several others. My early years influenced me to consider Poland a utopia, and even the war did not adversely affect or alter my sentimental attachments. There were no more ghosts left behind. I had seen it all once again and buried the remembrances of things past. Returning to the United States felt like revisiting heaven!

However, it was not that easy. A few years later I travelled to Frombork, a small town located on the Baltic coast near Stuthoff. I could not bring myself to visit the camp museum there. I was standing at the shores of the Baltic Sea. It was a cloudy day in early November, and the water looked gray and forbidding. I could see before me all those women from the past, thousands of them, drowning at this place, being prodded with bayonets and forced into the water and shot. All at once the water in the sea was no longer gray and murky but red with blood, hands pleadingly reaching upward. I quickly turned away in horror. This nightmarish sight sickened me.

My Aunt Giza arrived here on January 25, 1944. It was a very cold day . . . the shallow water turned to ice, frozen around the women's bodies, burying them under its weight. Little Elzunia was lying on the ground somewhere not far from here. The now quiet and deserted beach was trampled upon by proud SS murderers who fulfilled one of the glorious missions of the great heroes of Nazi Germany.

My bus arrived. I asked the driver if he was here when there was a concentration camp in Stuthoff. No, he answered, he was originally from Wilno. He did not arrive at this place until the early fifties. There is hardly any one left from those days, he added, only resettled people from eastern Poland. Those old times were just past history: the Teutonic Knights' cathedrals, the castles, the Copernicus Study and the Stutthof Camp, were all gone.

I took a long last look at the sea. It was still gray and quiet, and the beach, lonely and abandoned. Was it history already? For me, not yet, not now.

Many of my disappointments, hardships and happy experiences were already those of the average American. I learned what it meant to lose a father who died from a heart attack and a mother who suffered a fatal stroke. I found out that these were devastating events and that one did not have to survive a war to learn about suffering. I experienced the high and low points of being a mother, and more recently the unbounded joy of becoming a grandmother. I adored my children, my daughter born in Germany right after the war and my son born in my newly adopted country. I even enjoyed my role as a student again, earning a B.A., M.A. and Ph.D. in art history, my first love. It was actually Tom's idea that I reenter school. He loved every moment of it.

It was quite easy for me to understand my refugee friends with whom no words were necessary. But it no longer meant that I liked them all. There were now walls between us occasioned largely by the different lives we presently led. I became more attached to my American friends for their good qualities and for our mutuality of interests.

The easiest time for me was and still is the pleasure of being with Tom. We understand each other intuitively. Our pride and joy was our children. We probably failed them in more ways than one. But we did try our best, and as my father would say, "One can only do one's best."

From all the mosaic pieces of our lives we had to choose for them certain ethical principles and teach them never to lose hope. We would try to influence them to be strong, well adjusted human beings, keeping our own past experiences from them during their young years. How we succeeded they alone would eventually have to judge; this will be their story to tell.

On the whole our lives have been successful. Only deep inside I wonder what that really means. The answer comes quickly—life has to go on for my children and grandchildren. It was my war, not theirs, that made me what I am.

# Appendix

. . . . .

*A letter written to me by my Mother (translation) on the day before she thought she was to be killed. Omitted words are illegible in the original.*

Drohobycz                                                        27.V.43

My dearest, beloved only child!

They started yesterday to liquidate the Jewish population in Boryslaw. We are expecting it to happen at any moment here. I should like then at last in this way, my darling, to say goodby to you.

Do not cry and do not despair when you learn about our deaths. Zosia met her end on 12, II, 1943, a day after her birthday. Walterek wrote that he was unable to cry. Who knows what is happening to him. My heart is breaking from the pain, realizing that I shall see you no longer, my little child! I loved you both so much. God took Doneczka from me while I am abandoning you. Destiny! They brought us to such a condition that we are saying, perhaps, we have in a way, lived long enough. You are young, my darling. Your whole life is ahead of you. I am asking God to spare you all the miseries. If the dead know who they have left on this earth in tears, then I will always be near you. I would like very much for you to study. I would wish that you could use your great abilities for your own good and for that of others. You are a true daughter of your father. Try to be as good, as righteous, and as giving as he is. But take good care of yourself. You are still so young and you have so little experience in life. Be very careful before you decide to share your life with some one else. Marry only when you really fall deeply in love. Do not marry without love, everything else is fleeting. Only love is constant until death. I still love your father as well as I loved him twenty-five years ago. Try to be a good and efficient wife and a most giving mother. If you do not work professionally, try to be an able housekeeper and to that end learn to use your abilities. I never did that, and I know that Daddy suffered for it. I loved you both more than life, and yet I was not a good mother. I travelled with Daddy and left you both with a governess. I was young, and I loved your Father so very much, and those two loves were not easy to unite.

You will probably remain without aunts; maybe one of your uncles or cousins will survive. Stay in touch with them, even the worst relative is better than a stranger. Also try to have girl friends. I have seen . . . who did not have family had . . . friends.

I hope that God will help Daddy to survive. They are presently trying to execute the women without "R." Ila, Elzunia and I do not have this letter. If only I could be sure that Daddy would remain with you and Lonek with Oles. If not, try to find him (Oles) in Boryslaw. I am including Walterek's letter. If God permits, and you do find him, be a sister to him.

Mr. . . . , with whom I am leaving this letter is a generous noble man, . . . will give advice . . . .

My dearest child I would give anything to be able to kiss and embrace you. May God take care of you. Until the last moment of my life I will be thinking of you. In my thoughts I embrace your face, and kiss your eyes, cheeks and lips.

Your mother.

*(I found this letter among the personal belongings of my mother after she died in 1969.*

*The coveted "R" that my father had, but not mother, on this crucial day, but she received it shortly after.*

*Two letters written by Walter to my parents before he was taken to Janowska.*

*Walter's first letter:*

Lwow, 30.IV.1943

My Dears,

I am surprised that you have not received any news from me. I wrote you a letter and a card. Unfortunately, I cannot report anything good. First, I lost my mother, Zosia. She was seized on the 12th of February, a day after her birthday. She had just obtained a job for which she paid with all the money she had. This job proved to be a "trap." Thus I remain completely alone. My financial situation is hopeless. I am without a penny. I have nothing more to sell. The last of my money was expended when I was ill. I suffered from typhus. I survived this sickness in a weakened condition. Quite often I cannot afford a piece of bread. I live on what I receive ... a watery soup and 20 gs of bread. Dearest, if you can help me, do it now. I do not know what your condition is. I assume they it is not too good, but you are probably better off than I am. Except for this ... nothing has changed. The furrier to whom you wrote was a watchman in "Malopolska" (offices of the oil company) on Batory Street and he knew my father and yourself. He is a very decent man and honest. Again, if you can, please send something immediately. I received your package and the 300 zlotys you sent by a messenger and I thank you very much. Lwow is now "Judenfrei." It means that there are no unemployed Jews there. The ghetto is called Judenlager. Take good care of yourself and stay in the barrack. I kiss you all.

Walter

*Walter's second letter:*

Lwow, 7.V.43

I received the 300 zlotys and the package you sent for which God should bless you. Unfortunately, the money did not last long.

We are four now, who share expenses. We are all without funds. I cannot separate, besides, there are always monies needed for contributions, rent, etc. My dear ones, I know that you do not have much on which to live from day to day . . . If you could only see how I look. My face is like a straight line. I am glad that my Zosia cannot see it.

I need shoes size 43. Except for this there is nothing new. We now work from 7 a.m. to 7 in the evening, which is very tiring. I live in a wooden barrack infested with bed-bugs which keep us awake. However, this is not the most serious complaint. The important thing is to have something to eat. Ironically, things became less costly. But unfortunately, not for me. Generally speaking people here have money and they are eating . . . However there are others like me. I do not laugh or whistle anymore. On the other hand though . . . I am thinking . . . in any possible way . . . I do not wish to upset you . . . any more, and there is nothing really joyful I can report.

I kiss you and I finish.

Walter

P.S. Do you possibly have an old pair of pajamas?

Walter


*A letter from my father written sometime after 25 Feb. 1944 sent to Oberammergau*


Dearest, beloved Krysienko:

We received your letter of 25.II.44. We sensed a sadness in it. Five years of war and misery are exhausting. Perhaps it will end soon and we can start new life. Then you will be able to choose, my darling, if you would like to become a draftsman, an architect, a housewife, or, taking advantage of the skills you are now learning, an owner of a sports hotel, or better yet—simply remaining your mother's and father's beloved daughter doing only whatever else you like. We were very disappointed to learn that you did not receive our packages. The things we sent were quite simple but we hoped that they would make you feel warmer and would ease your hardship. Among all the threads and pleats, we enclosed our hearts. The packages may not have arrived but the breath of our love could not disappear and we hope it reached you.

We are all living at the mercy of a capricious, but in the end, a determined Tereska [Russia]. Time passes while at work, walks, during speculations and discussions on how to attend the wedding of Tereska [liberation by the Russians]. Not all are interested in being there. Our family, of course, but those close to Gebickis [the Poles] and even Cholupas [the Ukrainians] will celebrate in absentia, all moving toward Alma [Krakow]. As you see, it is very lively here. Just to leave it all behind! You, my darling, hold on, for the time being, to Mietek [the Polish friend of my father to whom I was writing letters for my parents]. When your vacation time comes [end of war] we will meet at the doctor's place [Switzerland]. She knows me rather well and will accept you with open arms. [My father always hoped that the B'nai B'rith Organization would take care of me in Switzerland or anywhere else in the world!].

Jadzia [my mother] is still working in her assigned factory and I in mine. In the evening we do our housework. Housekeeping depends on using up the "norms" [food allowances], the rest we buy. If you are interested, I quote some prices: flour 30-40 zls, butter 190 zls, eggs about 3 zls. We are all well, as are the others. Oles' is growing up to be a capable boy. He writes very clever letters about his friends, the chickens—he gave each one of them a name—about the travels of Gulliver, or other stories which he often composes himself.

Elzunia is a big girl, she weighs 62 kgs. and influenced by her much older friend, states that she would like to be more grown up and points naively, with an appropriate gesture, to her hips.

Does Wacek [the bombardments of the Allies] often disturb you? Jadzia is always bothering me about it. From his last letter [from news] we gather that he is now becoming rather bothersome, but I hope he respects you.

> I embrace you, my beloved
> darling, and I kiss you.
>
> Your Mateusz [my father]

*My mother's postscript in the same letter:*

My darling,

You are in my thoughts day and night. I am afraid that Wacek [bombardments] are annoying you. I ask God to grant you all the best. You are my greatest treasure and love. I have but one great desire, to see you happy.

Caresses,

Jadwiga [mother]

*The last card I received in Oberammergau from my parents who sent it from their hiding place in Boryslaw.*

Boryslaw 27, May, 44

Dear Krysiu,

On a trip from Tarnopol toward the west [just to confuse possible readers other than myself] a short note with most salient thoughts. As we have not yet reached our destination [freed!] and do not as yet have an apartment, we cannot, of course, send you our address. From our many relatives and friends we have news that some of them found good apartments [hiding places] for themselves, most of the others were placed together, not too far from Elzunia's pre-war hometown [Auschwitz Concentration Camp near Krakow] where all are healthy.

As you advised, the parents of Helenka, [my parents] during their trip, stopped at Boryslaw at a friend of Stacia's [a Polish Christian women], where they were greeted hospitably. When they find a permanent place they will contact Helenka [me] directly or through the lady doctor [Switzerland]. She [I] should therefore not worry even if she does not receive any news. We do not meet with Mietek [a Polish friend of my parents'] any more. We ask that you do not forget him. Knowing how you dislike writing, communicate once a month or every six weeks [not to write too often]. He is a good and courageous boy.

We would very much like to see you as a happy daughter and loving wife, on your own. I kiss and embrace you.

Your Pa

*This card in fact, told me everything that was going on with my parents and relatives, but I did not understand it at all. We learned that my parents were in hiding, in the house of a Polish woman in Boryslaw, that some of our other relatives and friends also managed to find hiding places, and that all the others were in Auschwitz, still alive. It was only after the war, and after I met my parents that I could really understand the contents of this card.*

*This is a letter written by Oleś on 25 Sept. 1945, after the war had ended, when my parents and he were in Krakow and when he had just received the news that I was alive, married, and so on . . .*

*In this letter Oleś mentions that he is not attending school in Krakow, but does not explain why. The reason was that he was called the equivalent of "cursed Jew" by another child in the class. This one episode affected his entire future life.*

Dear Ludka!

You cannot imagine how much joy your letter brought me. After waiting such a long time for news from you, this evoked in us a great deal of happiness. We were as joyful as little children! [He was 9 or 10 years old.] I am glad that you got married and I would very much like to meet your husband. I am building a boat and will sail in it from the Tibar to the Dead Sea [Oles' counted on the fact that I would understand what he meant by it as my father noted on the side of the letter. The word "Palestine" does not appear in the entire contents!] I have much to tell you but I will not write about these matters. I am not going to school and Tom will also not be able to attend. Tuśko [my father] makes official trips to many towns and takes me with him. I went to Wroclaw, Nisa, Opol . . .

Judith and Jack are in Paris. I attended school in Drohobycz to the third grade and I was the best student in the whole class. I had all "5". In May of 1945 we left for Krakow. There I went to school for four days before the yearly semester ended and received a report card grade of one "very good", and the rest "good." I then went to school for one day in the fifth grade but I will no longer attend [another reference to the same unfortunate remark]. At the first opportunity I will go from Cracowii to Napoli to . . . .

I do not know if your parents will agree, although they would also prefer to send me away. Tusko is considering shipping me off to America but I do not want to go, but—perhaps. I do not know what to think about all that. I would like to leave Krakow as soon as possible. I cannot stand it here. I do not know why, but I just cannot. I am sending you an elephant token because I know how much you like those animals . . .

We live near the river Wista and we enjoy a beautiful scenic view over Wawel and the river, also the Debnicky bridge and the church of . . . . The altar of Wit Stworz will be returned to Krakow this month. I travelled by boat around Bielany and there saw the church of St. Kamedulow. I also visited the "Skalka Twardowski-ego" ("Twardowski Rock") and went to the church behind the rock. It was built in the XIIIth century in Gothic style. Goodbye, I kiss you hundreds of times.

Oles'

Best regards to Tom.

*First letter from Oles who is now in Palestine*

26,IV,1946

Dear Ludka,

I received your letter yesterday and I was thrilled to read it. I am the happiest person here. I live in a kibbutz where I study and play. . . . It is Paradise on earth here. Jews are managers, policemen, drivers, as well as workers and physicians. . . .

I have already visited nearly the entire country through numerous excursions. I was at the Sea of Galilee, I visited all the kibbutzim there and the ruins of old Israeli towns. I saw scorpions, snails and a great variety of fish there. I am now able to communicate in Hebrew and the words I speak I can also write, almost without mistakes. Try to come here as soon as you can.

I enjoyed the sea trip very much and the more the ship rolled, the more my pleasure increased. I was not seasick at all, and ate enough for two. Near Crete we ran into a terrible storm and the whole crew was on alert. I liked Marseille very much and saw all that one could possibly see there. At first I was disappointed with Paris. Since, from the many accounts I read, I expected it to be more beautiful, but on the following day I changed my mind and loved it very much.

Many kisses for you and your husband.

Your Oles

*My aunt Judith (Dita) wrote the following account:*

I do not remember the exact time, but it seems to me that at the beginning of May 1943 a rumor spread that the ghetto in Drohobycz would be liquidated. My parents were already in a hiding place that my sister Ila's husband Dolek built, and where he, Ila and Elzunia were to hide if and when a final liquidation of the Jews was to take place.

I decided then to join my husband Jack, who was working in a lumber yard at Herawka, a suburb on the outskirts of Drohobycz. For me, this step was quite painful and difficult to take as I would be separated from the rest of my family. Still, it was a change for the better. The air was invigorating there and we also had lots of freedom to move around. We were in a camp with 200 young boys and girls. We had adequate food and we were deluding ourselves by believing that perhaps we would be allowed to remain here until the end of the war. But the Germans decided otherwise. On July 20, 1943, at 4 o'clock in the morning, we heard cars approaching and the barking of dogs. Shortly after, there were rappings on all the doors and men announcing an immediate "Appel." The whole camp was already surrounded by soldiers and dogs. We were all taken to the prison in Drohobycz. My oldest sister Amalia, who returned to camp after spending a few months on the Aryan side of Lwow, was then working as a secretary for the German commander of the camp, SA man Hechtsmann. His attitude toward the Jews was relatively good, and he greatly respected my sister. Throughout my life my sister Amalia was my guarding and guiding angel, and now she also saved my husband and myself. When she learned that we were sent to prison, she begged Hechtmann for help. He immediately ordered our release. Through other inter-mediaries about another fifteen people were saved. The rest were shot in trenches. Earlier, when I entered the cell, I saw on the wall in my mother's hand, "Anna and Gustav. After 10 days of torment we are going to our death." I then took a pencil and wrote a post-script: "Judith, your youngest daughter, is going with you." A few minutes later my husband and I were freed. This is how I discovered how my beloved parents' lives had ended. The pain I felt then, is still with me.

After we left the prison we were told to go to the work camp where the rest of my family was staying. My oldest sister Amalia, my sister Gizela with their husbands, and Ila with her husband and their 14-year-old daughter Elzunia were there. My husband Jack was assigned to do office work. I was sent to the kitchen.

While at Herawka, Jack, who spent nearly his entire life in Paris, became friendly with a farmer who had previously lived in France. Both of them would often speak in French. The man owned a small farm and mentioned to Jack that if the need arose, he would hide the both of us. A month later, on the 28th of March, 1944, as the Soviets were approaching Little Poland, and afraid that the liquidation of the Jewish work camp would soon take place, Jack and I, when returning from work, tore off our star of David arm-bands and went off into another part of town. It was 5 p.m. and we walked until 10 o'clock at night. When it was completely dark we went to the farm. There, the farmer made room for us in the stable, which also housed two cows, one horse and a few pigs. A small area in the barn was set aside, covered with straw, and that was our hiding place. My oldest sister Amalia and her husband also found a hiding place in Boryslaw. They were approached earlier by a woman employee of my brother-in-law. He had done a favor for her while he was a director of the oil company "Malopolska" in Boryslaw. The woman, sanctioned by the Polish underground, offered to hide them in her attic. In camp, at that time, there were my sister Gizela with her husband Leon, who intended to go into hiding sometime later, my brother-in-law Dolek, Ila's husband and little Elzunia. My sister Ila was condemned to death a long time ago on August 27, 1943. Dolek and Elzunia had no hiding place since the one that Dolek built was discovered by the Gestapo a month earlier while my parents were there.

We were unable to stand upright in our small space; we could only lie or sit. We could not light a candle because straw was strewn around. Our farmer would bring us food twice a day, but only one glass of water which was supposed to be sufficient for washing. We shared our small space with two young men.

After two weeks, our farmer told us that we must leave because the Soviets were retreating and the war, in his opinion, might last for a long time. All our pleading was in vain, and on April 14 (my sister Giza's birthday) at 6 o'clock in the morning we started towards the camp. From a distance we could see that the grounds were surrounded by cannons and dogs. We passed them near the camp without stopping. We noticed Leon helping my sister Giza into the truck. My heart was breaking, but again we did not stop, because we could not help them or anyone else. They spotted us, as Lonek, who survived the concentration camps, told us nearly a year and a half later. Giza never returned.

That gruesome day we walked through the town the whole day long, without food, terrified, not daring to rest, so as not to direct attention to ourselves. We were afraid to get too close to anyone because we smelled of cows. Not until dark did we dare risk going back to our farm. The owner was already asleep so we returned to our hiding place. Terrified, we waited to hear what he would say in the morning when he saw us. Thank God he was a pious man, and his reaction was that the Almighty must have wanted to save us, and for that reason he had to continue to help us. During the next month, he was apprehensive at times, even angry and he would then tell us that all the hidden Jews in the neighborhood had already been murdered. Sometimes, when he was in a good mood he would tell us that the Germans were retreating and how wonderful the approaching Soviets were. As time passed he gave us less and less to eat, and what was even worse, hardly any water with which to wash. Still we survived there in much better condition than did many others.

In the fifth month, on the sixth of August (my niece Ludka's birthday) at five in the morning the Soviets arrived, and our misery ended. On the next day Jack and I travelled the 9 kilometers to

Boryslaw to find out if my sister Amalia and her husband had survived. We found them in poor health, but they were there, and all four of us, with heavy hearts and lowly spirits and with little physical strenth, left ready to start a new life.

*Epilogue to "Janowska Camp"*

While at Janowska I never thought that my job was of any importance. It was only much later, when I was out of the concentration camp, that I received a letter from my girl friend with whom I attended the Architectural School in 1941—a letter which was an eye-opener for me. Niusia found out that I used to register the inmates while I worked at Janowska. She begged me to advise her on how to change the job of her fiance who was recently brought into camp. She wrote that he was assigned to physical labor, much beyond his powers of endurance and strength. It could kill him within weeks. Most horrifying, however, was the news that the man who replaced me was taking bribes for special favors in job assignments. She wanted me to tell her how to approach him, or if I thought that she should beg him for help. I knew the man quite well, and it never would have occurred to me that he, or anyone else, would take advantage of those terrified human beings in their most frightened time when they were first brought into that hell on earth. I knew those moments well. I could see their faces in my mind's eye, their hesitation, their despair which still haunts me. God, I thought, I never realized while in camp, that I could have helped or harmed the inmates. I knew so little, not only then, but throughout the long war.

*"Little" Mary's story*

It was not untill 1964 when little Mary and I met on a holiday in Rome, that I heard her story for the first time. She related it briefly. It was early in 1943 when she, then a fourteen- or fifteen-year-old teen-ager, and a few other girls who were about her age were summoned every day from the Lwow ghetto to Janowska camp where

they would meet in a room without having to perform any assigned
tasks. They would be provided with the best food possible at that
time along with plenty of nice clothes. Obersturmfuehrer Gebauer
himself checked if they were receiving whatever they more or
less wished. In time, though, Mary noticed that periodically (every
few weeks) one of the girls would disappear. She told this to friends
of her family with whom she was staying (her parents were gone by
then in a previous selection). They bought Aryan papers for her,
and registered her for work in Germany. It was another aspect of
Janowska camp of which I was never aware. How many others
were there? How many witnesses were gone forever without telling
their story?

*"Big" Mary's Story*

*Dear, I don't know . . . Krysienko . . . or Ludka . . . or what? . . . do
you know when a person starts writing memoirs? Apparently when
they grow old, suffer from sclerosis and when their memory fails. . .*

LWOW, end of May, 1943

I came to Janowska camp where all workers who were leaving
for Germany were ordered to assemble. Through a loudspeaker it
was announced that those who understood German should come
to the office to pick up working papers and tickets for five persons
who were travelling in the same direction. I collected the papers
for the five of us who were going to Bavaria. Later, our group had
to submit to delousing. We were first in line. Stripped, we walked
through halls crowded with Ukrainian police and civilians, several
SS men. You, my poor darling, were walking right behind me. You
had a headache, you were sick and you were incredibly brave to
leave for Germany in this condition. You looked like a picture of
five Jewish girls combined in one. Have you ever heard of a young
Polish working girl suffering from a migraine headache as you

claimed you had? At the railroad station I noticed that you had some problems with a Ukrainian. But soon the train started to move. I came closer to you and said "wus epes Kristine", which was a Yiddish idiomatic question "how are you Kristine" but neither I nor you knew any Yiddish. I then whispered in Polish how happy I was that you were travelling on this transport because I was Jewish too. Our joy was boundless but guarded as there were other people around us. You, my darling, told me that you were terribly afraid that I was a denouncer or just an anti-semite. But then even your headache seemed to vanish. We started to evaluate our companions. There were about three hundred workers going to Germany, men, women, young and middle-aged. We were sitting in one compartment with the five girls who were bound for Bavaria. The sun rays beamed on the pocketbook of a girl, who was the youngest in our group, named Mary. The light revealed traces of a monogram "P.S." We immediately started to guess out what her real name might be. Definitely not Mary. This girl, when she noticed while in Lwow, that a Ukrainian was very rude, quickly stood up and said that she had to go back home to see her uncle. She panicked. I went after her and told her that she couldn't go as I already had her train ticket. After much hesitation, she remained . . .

After many train jumpings our group boarded one bound for Vienna. There were still the five of us. A third, was Mary who did not open her mouth throughout the trip, and while in Vienna, disappeared. She was probably one of us. The fourth girl, Hanka, was definitely not Jewish. When she awakened next morning and saw the white peaks of the Alps she exclaimed: "Jesus, Maria, am I in heaven?" There was also a Victoria who gave me a cropped picture of herself. Near her probably was her Jewish looking husband. We could easily have had a "minyan", but of women.

In 1944 I left Germany for Prague with a Czech husband. On the day the war ended I told him that I was Jewish. He was cooking a soup then and asked for the salt. I told him, "Stop cooking for a moment, what I am telling you is more important." He answered, "but where did you put the salt?" I screamed, "you did not hear me, I am Jewish" and he again said, "Sakra slysim, kde mas tu sul?" ("Hell, I heard you but where have you put the salt?") And so I was standing there and thinking that all those long years of running and hiding were nothing compared to his salt! The war was over . . .

*A letter from my father's cousin received in November 1958*

. . . To your question who were the Poles and Ukrainians who saved the Jews in Boryslaw?, I can answer that they were not members of the educated class who organized or were willing to endanger their lives for the Jews. While they did not actively work against us as a class, they certainly did not help. (Of course, there were exceptions.) Usually, the Jews were aided by the working class (but again, some would denounce them). My wife, her aunt, and I were saved by a Polish man and his Ukrainian wife, whose livelihood during this period was implemented by stealing cows and calves and slaughtering them in the back of their house, adjacent to a small storage room where we were hiding. The Germans were constantly passing around the house and even entering it as the owner had two pretty daughters. The whole family kept trembling from fear that the Germans would discover us. If we were discovered, it would mean death for all. I remember that his wife was begging him to relocate us, as she was on the verge of a nervous breakdown, but the man's answer always was: "I promised to save them, and I have to keep my word". Of course, we were paying him as long as our money lasted. Toward the end, when it was all gone, he still sheltered and saved us . . .